FUN AND GAINS

To my mother and father, Jacquelin Hart and Harrison Hart

I love you

CAROLYN GREENWICH

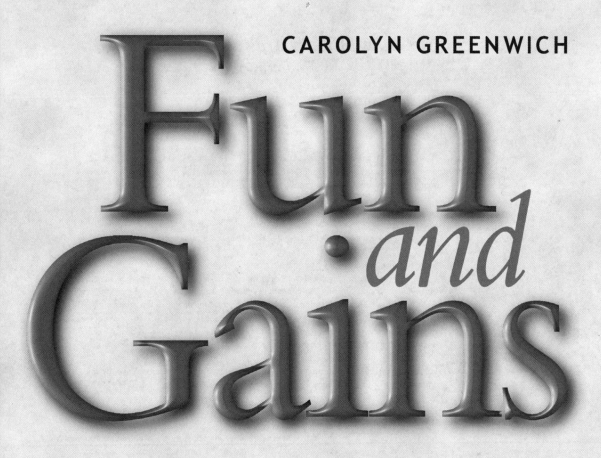

Fun *and* Gains

Motivate and Energize Staff
with Workplace Games, Contests and Activities

The McGraw-Hill Companies, Inc.

Sydney New York San Francisco Auckland
Bangkok Bogotá Caracas Hong Kong
Kuala Lumpur Lisbon London Madrid
Mexico City Milan New Delhi San Juan
Seoul Singapore Taipei Toronto

McGraw·Hill Australia

A Division of The McGraw·Hill Companies

McGraw-Hill books are available at special quantity discounts to use as premiums and sales promotions, or for use in corporate training programs. For more information, please contact the Special Sales Manager, Professional Publishing and Education Division, at the address below.

National Library of Australia Cataloguing-in-Publication data:

Greenwich, Carolyn.
Fun and gains: motivate and energize staff with workplace games, contests and activities.

ISBN 0 074 70770 1.

1. Employees—Training of—Problems, exercises, etc. 2. Employee motivation. 3. Creative ability—Problems, exercises, etc. 4. Creative thinking—Problems, exercises, etc. I. Title.

658.3124

Published in Australia by
McGraw-Hill Book Company Australia Pty Limited
4 Barcoo Street, Roseville NSW 2069, Australia
Acquisitions Editor: Meiling Voon
Production Editor: Megan Lowe
Editor: Caroline Hunter, Burrumundi Partnership
Designer: RTJ Klinkhamer
Cover designer: RTJ Klinkhamer
Typeset in 12/14 Sabon by RTJ Klinkhamer
Printed on 80 gsm woodfree by Prowell Productions, Hong Kong

Contents

4 EFFECTIVE COMMUNICATION

How to Use This Book

There is nothing that succeeds like success! *Fun and Gains* is a collection of workplace games, sales contests and activities that have been used by managers and staff in organizations to achieve gains through fun. 'Fun' is an important element in the workplace. People learn and achieve more when the process is enjoyable. Fun activities motivate and energize, and make results easier to achieve for all. I hope the successes of the contributors to *Fun and Gains* become your successes.

Fun and Gains is divided into 4 important areas where gains are crucial:
• Winning Attitudes
• Reinforcing Professionalism
• Achieving Greater Sales
• Effective Communication

The *Winning Attitudes* activities in *Fun and Gains* have helped organizations to improve morale and maintain a positive outlook. Winning attitudes make the workplace a joy to work in. Effective managers know that it all starts with your attitude. You can never have a bad day with a good attitude. Successful managers always strive to create and maintain positive morale to avoid apathy and negativity creeping into the workplace. We live in an era of rapid change, therefore we have to keep changing our techniques to keep stimulating people's enthusiasm and optimism. In this section, you will find a variety of activities that help achieve winning attitudes.

Reinforcing Professionalism is vital. People can slip into bad habits and not even realize it. In this section, there are a number of activities that will help maintain standards of behavior. The activities will help improve leadership, work practices, product knowledge, reliability and time management. Various things can happen that cause staff to act in ways that are unprofessional. Instead of punishing people when they are unprofessional, it is more productive to focus on the solution. In *Reinforcing Professionalism* you will find a series of activities that managers have used to bring out the best in people.

Achieving Greater Sales is the quest of every company. Imagine your staff increasing sales by 50% in a month, simply by playing a game that costs $50. Or imagine customer service staff who were afraid of selling suddenly becoming enthusiastic and successful at cross-selling. These are the types of results that managers have achieved through creating simple sales contests and fun games. The sales contests can be used in call centers, branches or retail outlets. The contests are varied and are designed to increase sales results through sales conversions, cross-selling, up-selling, lead generation or referrals.

Effective Communication is vital to the success of any organization. Communication is a skill that can be improved with constant attention and continual development. The objective of all communication, whether speaking to customers, staff or colleagues, is to achieve a positive response. Included in this section are some games, classroom training exercises and on-the-job training techniques to enhance communication with co-workers and customers.

The ideas in this book can be adapted easily to suit almost any office situation. Simply consider your objectives and the interests and personalities of the people in the office. Remember, fun can mean different things to different people.

For easy reference, the book follows a set format. Under each activity, the information is given under the following headings:
- Purpose
- Group Size
- Resource
- Method
- Reward/prize
- Benefit
- Source

Special thanks to the managers, team leaders, consultants and trainers whose workplace games, sales contests and activities have made this book possible. The contributor of each activity can be found in the Contributors section at end of the book.

Thanks also to all the readers and contributors of *The Fun Factor: games, sales contests and activities that make work fun and get results*. *The Fun Factor* continues to help people to achieve incredible results.

As always, I am already planning the next book and I would love to hear from you. What workplace activities have you used that have achieved great results? Please call or e-mail me.

If your company is seeking a conference presentation or a training program in any of these areas—'Achieving Greater Sales', 'Customer Service as a Competitive Tool', 'High Gain Communication' and 'Motivate and Energize your Staff'—please give me a call. I would love to talk to you.

Best of luck with your fun and gains.

Carolyn Greenwich
carolyn@winningattitudes.com
Tel: (61) 2 9241 1361

1 WINNING
ATTITUDES

It all starts with your attitude. You can never have a bad day if you have a good attitude. A manager's job is to create and maintain winning attitudes and not allow apathy and negativity to creep into the workplace.

We live in an era when there are new movies, new books and new songs every month, and this means that we have to keep changing our techniques to keep stimulating those winning attitudes among our staff.

Motivator of the Week

It is very difficult to come up with new motivational ideas each week to stimulate your team. Share the fun and responsibility by getting team members to create their own motivational strategies.

PURPOSE
• To have a new strategy each week to stimulate positive attitudes in the team or to help boost the team's productivity

GROUP SIZE
Ideal for a team of 6 to 14 people

RESOURCE
Provide a small budget of $10 to be spent however the 'Motivator of the Week' wishes to use the budget to achieve the results (they may wish to spend the money on prizes, visual reinforcements or a combination of both)

METHOD
Each week, select a different team member to be in charge of motivating. Give them as much freedom as possible. Let them decide what outcome they would like to achieve by the game, activity or contest that they are creating. They may wish to boost positive attitudes, improve professionalism, enhance communication or increase sales or productivity in a particular area.

Show them the section 'Create Your Own Game' on pages 157–60. Or provide them with a copy of *The Fun Factor* or other books on motivation for ideas.

The 'Motivator of the Week' will need to consider their fellow team members' interests and motivations. In doing so, they are more likely to come up with some very clever ideas that will help stimulate the team and boost morale.

When each person in the team has had a turn at being the 'Motivator of the Week', hold a competition to see which activities were the most popular and the most effective. Ask the team members to vote on their favorite motivational activities by giving 3 points for first choice, 2 points for second choice and 1 point for third choice.

PRIZE   A certificate for the top 3 winners of the motivational activities (see page 4) with prizes worth $50, $30 and $20. The amount of prize money and the $10 a week budget will be a small price to pay for the benefits your company reaps.

BENEFIT   • Your staff will start to take responsibility for maintaining positive attitudes
   • You will develop a series of motivational activities that you can use in the future
   • You can share the most popular and effective activities with other companies by sending me details about the game for publication in the next motivational book

SOURCE   Carolyn Greenwich

Motivator of the Week

Name _____

Construction Worker Theme Day

Many companies have to endure the inconvenience and noise of office remodeling. Rather than listening to staff complain, turn this negative event into a fun day that will be remembered by all!

PURPOSE
- To liven up spirits in the office and let people know that having fun is better than complaining

GROUP SIZE
10 to 100 people

RESOURCE
Hard hats

METHOD
Announce to the staff that, due to the construction chaos in the office, everyone will be asked to dress accordingly in construction clothing on a designated day. Tell staff that the more authentic the better, and assure them that all managers in the department will be participating enthusiastically.

This technique worked so well in one call center that staff showed up in overalls or work shorts, with fake tattoos on their arms, cigarette packs rolled up in their T-shirt sleeves and tool belts around their waists. Some of the females wore fake moustaches, beards and wigs. A few people brought their lunch in a tool box. One staff member brought in a plank of wood and several brought in tools to decorate their desks. While hard hats were provided, most people chose to wear their own hard hats or headgear.

In the afternoon, find a staff member from another department who is very big and muscular or perhaps a keen body builder. Ask him to dress appropriately in construction clothing and get him to come through the department or call center to hand out soft drinks to all the staff.

BENEFIT
- Provides a clear demonstration to staff of turning a negative into a positive
- Reduces stress and creates happier staff
- Allows people to show off their creativity

SOURCE
Darren Hauschild

The Toy Box

Childhood memories can be easily rekindled to help reduce stress and lift spirits. This simple activity will bring a smile to the face of even the most negative person in the office.

PURPOSE
- To introduce an element of fun and humor therapy into the workplace

GROUP SIZE 8 to 25 people

RESOURCE A large toy box painted in cheerful colors and designs

METHOD Ask each team member to bring in a toy for the toy box. Examples of toys that will bring a smile to anyone's face include:
1. a talking doll
2. a stuffed animal
3. juggling balls
4. pick-up sticks
5. toy eggs
6. a jack in the box
7. a barrel of monkeys
8. a toy tool kit

Locate the toy box in a handy place. Tell the team members that, whenever they are stressed or in need of a break, they can select a toy to amuse themselves with.

BENEFIT
- Creates the fun of childhood memories
- Gets everyone involved in creating a happy office

SOURCE Sarah Wade

Fabulous Food Friday

This activity can be introduced to create a bit of fun and camaraderie in the office. While it may be feared that productivity could suffer, experience has proven that productivity is actually increased when staff have an event to look forward to.

PURPOSE
- To build team spirit, have fun and help people learn more about each other

GROUP SIZE Up to 30 people

RESOURCE A large table or counter, paper plates, napkins, plastic spoon, forks, knives and cups

METHOD On 'Fabulous Food Friday', invite everyone to bring in their favorite dish. Any type of food or beverage is allowed (except alcohol). Place all the food on a table in the morning, and write the name of the person who brought the particular food next to their dish.

During the day, invite staff to help themselves to the vast selection of food any time they feel like a snack. Staff will enjoy sampling the different foods and complimenting each other on their culinary talents.

REWARD Lots of anticipation as the day approaches. Great fun and enjoyment for all on the day.

BENEFIT
- Provides an easy way to socialize
- Gives staff an opportunity to get to know each other better
- Reduces stress

SOURCE Susie James Brown

The Birthday Zone

For most people in an organization, their birthday is a very important day of the year. However, celebrating each person's birthday can become routine instead of special. Here is a fun way to make everyone feel special and to give them an event to look forward to.

PURPOSE • To celebrate everyone's birthday in an extra special manner

GROUP SIZE 8 to 20 people

RESOURCE $50 for a special birthday cake

METHOD Divide the office into birthday zones so that you have an equal number of people whose birthdays fall in each zone. For example, you may have 10 people in the office whose birthdays fall within January and February and 10 whose birthdays fall within March, April and May.

Ask each zone to elect a group of 3 people who will organize their birthday party outside of office hours. It is up to these people to find a consensus on how everyone would like to celebrate their birthday. The company will pay $50 for a birthday cake for the party. The event should meet the budget of those people who are involved. Examples of events might include:

1. going out for dinner or breakfast
2. going bowling, dancing or horse riding
3. holding a barbecue or picnic in the park
4. organizing a party at someone's house

To add hilarity and fun to the party, suggest that they play the Birthday Exchange Game. This game is always enjoyable. Each person buys a mystery gift for approximately $10. Alternatively, each person brings a 'white elephant gift' from home (this is something that they own but never use). All gifts are wrapped. At the party each person draws a number. The person who draws number one selects the first gift. The person who draws number two can select a gift or take the gift off the person who drew number one. If a gift is taken off a person, then that person selects again from the pile of gifts. This process continues so that the person who draws the highest number can select the last gift or choose from any of the gifts that have already be selected and unwrapped.

REWARD Birthday certificate (see page 10) given on day of birthday

BENEFIT • A great way to help people to get to know others in the office
• Lets everyone know when each person's birthday is
• Avoids the routine office birthday cake celebration

SOURCE Carolyn Greenwich and Linda Urquhart

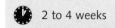

The Stock Market Game

This is a popular game to play if staff are interested in the stock market. It was so popular with a group of client service officers that they created a second version of the game (see below) to help them on a special outbound telephone campaign to existing customers.

PURPOSE
- To create fun and interest in the office
- To help get through the workload more easily

GROUP SIZE   Teams of 4 to 6 people

RESOURCE   Newspaper or Internet access to check stock market prices

Version 1

METHOD   Assign an independent person the task of monitoring the Stock Market Game. Each team starts with a pretend amount of $100 000 in cash. During the period of the game the team can choose to invest in any particular stocks that it wishes. The first 10 trades that the team makes during the time frame of the game are free. After this, each trade costs $50. All trades need to be registered with the game monitor and can only be made during a break or at lunchtime.

   At the end of the game, the team with the most valuable portfolio of stocks is declared the winner. The other teams must provide the prize for the winning team.

PRIZE   This should be decided before the game starts. Everyone may decide to pitch in a dollar to play the game, and all the proceeds go to the winning team to spend how it wishes. Or everyone may decide to provide a special afternoon tea for the winning team.

Version 2

Version 1 of this game was so popular with the client service officers that they decided to incorporate the game into a campaign. The client service officers needed to contact 2500 clients to provide them with information. To make it more interesting to make these outbound calls and reach the clients they created this version of the game.

METHOD Each time a client service officer calls and speaks to 5 clients they receive $100 pretend money for their team. At the end of the day the team meets to discuss how it will invest the pretend money made that day. The team is able to choose between 10 stocks that were chosen before the game started. These stocks were chosen because they were considered to be volatile stocks. If the team does not wish to invest in the stocks, it can hold on to its cash. All trades need to be registered with the stock market game monitor. There is no charge for a trade.

The game ends either at the end of the time frame when all calls should have been made, or when all calls have been made. At the end of the game, the team with the highest dollar value portfolio wins.

PRIZE $50 to $100 for the winning team to celebrate its victory

BENEFIT • Helps staff to learn more about the stock market
• Motivates staff to achieve so they can have more dollars to play the game
• Makes it easy and fun to accomplish the goal

SOURCE Avril Ward; Tracey Flynn

Santa Claus is Coming

The key to this activity is the element of surprise on the last day of work before Christmas. Everyone will be looking forward to the exchange of gifts, but they will not anticipate the fun and laughter that will be created in the process.

PURPOSE
- To organize gift-giving at Christmas time in a simple, inexpensive and fun way

GROUP SIZE   8 to 35 people

RESOURCE   A list of the names of each staff member and the type of gift (between $5 and $10) that they would like (if they do not wish to specify, they can write 'surprise me'), and a Christmas card for each person to attach to their gift (see page 14)

METHOD   Once the office Christmas tree is up, put all the staff names into a hat and ask everyone to draw out a name—this will be the person for whom they will be buying a Christmas gift. The gift-givers should always remain anonymous. Each gift-giver is given a card to attach to their gift that says: Merry Christmas to (name of person), from Santa Claus.

As gifts are purchased and wrapped they can be placed under the Christmas tree for the time leading up to Christmas.

Do not let any staff members know how the gifts will be distributed. In the afternoon of the last working day before Christmas, ask one of the managers to dress up as Santa Claus and suddenly appear in the office. As staff continue to work, Santa makes his way around to each staff member, giving them their present and having his photo taken with them by polaroid camera. Staff may choose to sit on his lap, hug him, stand next to him or have Santa sit on their lap.

BENEFIT
- The element of surprise will give everyone a lift
- A personal photo with Santa will bring back happy childhood memories

SOURCE   Darren Hauschild

Merry Xmas

To _____

from Santa Claus

Merry Xmas

To _____

from Santa Claus

Spring Bonnet Surprise

A very brave manager with an outrageous sense of fun is needed for this morale-boosting celebration day. This activity brought tears of laughter to everyone's eyes in the customer service center of an energy company.

PURPOSE
• To celebrate Easter or Spring and to lift the spirits of the staff

GROUP SIZE
20 to 80 people

RESOURCE
Easter eggs

METHOD
Announce to your staff that you will be having a Spring bonnet (or Easter bonnet) competition. The prizes should be attractive enough so that even the diehards will participate. Have 3 prizes such as Most Creative Hat, Most Humorous Hat and Best Hat.

Inform everyone that part of the condition of winning the prize is that they will have to wear their bonnet all day. If staff are in an office situation where they see customers face to face, it will make the customers smile. If staff only deal with customers over the phone, it will give everyone in the office a chance to see and enjoy the bonnets throughout the day.

Ask a male manager or team leader to dress up as a 'playboy' bunny. Go wild with the cross-dressing. The more outrageous the better. In the afternoon, when the fun and excitement of the bonnets is starting to wear off, turn on some seductive music and surprise the staff with the entrance of the playboy bunny. Provide the playboy bunny with a supply of Easter eggs to hand out to all staff members as he makes his way around the office.

PRIZE
Best Hat wins dinner for two; Most Creative Hat wins a large Easter basket; and Most Humorous Hat wins champagne and 2 movie tickets. Give certificates to the winners (see page 16).

BENEFIT
• You will have created a day to be remembered
• Staff will feel appreciated because their manager went to so much effort to create a fun day

SOURCE
Darren Hauschild

BEST HAT

_____

MOST
CREATIVE HAT

_____

MOST
HUMOROUS HAT

_____

Mellow Yellow

The staff and manager of a large newspaper call center with over 200 staff wanted to cheer everyone up. What better way to do it than to turn the entire center into a blaze of yellow?

PURPOSE
- To boost the spirits and energy of the staff
- To welcome the season of Spring into the office

GROUP SIZE Any number of people

RESOURCE Anything that is gold or yellow

METHOD Announce to the staff that the theme for the day or the week is yellow. Split the staff into teams and ask each of the teams to pick a theme and a team name for the week that has to do with the color yellow. Examples include: The Bumble Bees, The Daffodils, Sunshine and The Lemons. Once the teams have their theme, encourage them to decorate their areas to reflect their chosen theme during the week or in preparation for the theme day.

In the morning, as people are coming to work, play music that has the word yellow in it, such as 'Mellow Yellow' or 'Tie a Yellow Ribbon Round the Old Oak Tree'.

On the theme day or the last day of the theme week, ask everyone to dress in the color yellow. Serve a morning or afternoon tea that is all yellow in color, serving food such as lemon cakes or lemon cookies, cheese and crackers, yellow fruit and lemonade. Ask each team to provide a portion of the morning or afternoon tea.

PRIZE Prizes are not necessary—the fun is sufficient. If you wish to invite a guest from another department or a top executive, you may like to ask the guest to judge the best yellow outfit or the best team decoration. Select a prize that is yellow in color, such as a bouquet of flowers, for the best outfit and a yellow box of chocolates, such as Whitman's samplers, for the winning team.

BENEFIT
- Stimulates a great deal of good feeling among staff members
- Helps reduce stress levels in the office

SOURCE Sandra Lau

17

Lots of Balls

This is an energetic group activity in which everyone participates. It is very loud and a lot of fun. It can be used during the day to energize staff or at team meetings as an icebreaker. One team member commented at the conclusion of the activity that they did not realize that they could learn so much from a game.

PURPOSE
- To lift the spirits of the team and to show them how important teamwork really is

GROUP SIZE The bigger the better

RESOURCE Lots of space, CD or cassette player, lively music and soft objects

METHOD
1. Explain what you are all about to embark on—this is an energizing activity that requires teamwork. Participants form a circle and throw soft objects, such as Nerf balls, soft rubber balls, beach balls or a mixture of these, to one another while energetic music plays. The objective is to keep all the balls from dropping. Everyone should have equal involvement.
2. Provide a practice run with one ball and no music. Then add the music and start to introduce more balls.
3. Enjoy!
4. Be prepared to be the 'party pooper' when you bring the activity to a close.
5. If this game is to be used for team-building purposes, then debrief the staff afterwards by discussing how the group worked together as a team. Were the guidelines adhered to? If not, why not? This activity can be tied into how people function in teams at work.

BENEFIT
- Creates participants who are happy, smiling, full of life and have good feelings about their colleagues and work
- Helps staff to understand the important outcomes of teamwork

SOURCE Robyn Woodgate

Anniversary

Retaining top staff is always a challenge. Often, people leave their job because they feel unappreciated. Or they may stay, but leave 'mentally' if they do not feel recognized and appreciated. There are many opportunities that provide quick and easy ways to appreciate your staff that you do not want to miss, starting with celebrating their anniversary with the organization.

PURPOSE • Acknowledgment and appreciation of years of service

RESOURCE A list of the commencement dates of every staff member in your office and anniversary cards or certificates (see page 20)

METHOD On the morning of the staff member's anniversary, make a short presentation to them, ideally in front of other staff members. Thank them for their work over the last year and acknowledge 3 to 5 specific accomplishments. To add in a bit of laughter, relate the most humorous moment they brought to the office. Present them with the card and small gift.

REWARD Card and small gift, such as a small box of chocolates

BENEFIT • Lifts everyone's morale
• Makes that particular staff member feel very important

SOURCE Tracy Tozer

Happy Anniversary

_____

Congratulations on your

_____

year at

_____

Hallowe'en Happenings

Hallowe'en is a perfect time for an energy boost. This time of the year can be a flat period before the Christmas rush. This activity is a great way to lift your team out of the plateau that can occur after a long period of increasing sales. The increase in sales and productivity far outweighs the cost of the day. The activity proves that having fun gets exciting results.

PURPOSE
• To lift morale and lay the foundations for increased productivity

GROUP SIZE
15 to 25 people

RESOURCE
Decorations and costumes, and candy

METHOD
To prepare for Hallowe'en Happenings, here are a few guidelines:

1. *Costume choosing expedition:* Take a small group at a time to a costume shop and pay for half the price of their costume hire—this will encourage staff to choose elaborate costumes.

2. *The boss's costume:* Let the team choose the boss's costume. Do not be surprised at their choice (Cheryl's team chose the 'Grim Reaper' for her!).

3. *Rev up the clients:* Send spooky faxes to your best customers telling them that Hallowe'en is a great day to place an order, as they can be part of the Hallowe'en event (see page 23). Call clients who have not placed an order for a while. Let them know what is happening and invite them to place an order on Hallowe'en.

4. *Decoration planning:* Plan on making a real splash. Get everyone involved with planning, providing or purchasing the decorations. Use lunchtimes for decoration shopping expeditions.

To make the event exciting, decorate everything after work the night before Hallowe'en. Decorate staff's workstations with cobwebs, spiders, etc. Get everyone to agree to come to work fully dressed. With all the build-up to the customers over the previous few weeks, the phones will start ringing with orders.

With a great reason to call, it also makes those outbound calls more fun and effective.

Take as many photos as you can. Send some to clients. If they have not met the staff personally, they will not be able to forget them now.

REWARD Lots of Hallowe'en candy available to all on the day

BENEFIT • An immediate increase in sales and morale
• Encourages external staff to apply for jobs in your department (a fun place to work)

SOURCE Cheryl Dooley and Stephen Dooley

Happy HALLOWE'EN

It's all happening at

_____

We're here to help you. Give us a call on

_____

Scarecrow Competition

What better way to scare off any blue or negative feelings in the office than to have scarecrows in the office to do it for you?

PURPOSE • To use the creative energy in the office to boost morale

GROUP SIZE Any number of people (for a small office you would probably create just 1 scarecrow, but for a large call center you may have as many as 20 scarecrows)

RESOURCE A few bales of hay to share between the teams (all other resources required to make the scarecrows are provided by the staff)

METHOD Announce the scarecrow competition at the beginning of the month (see flier on page 25). Divide the office into teams or use the teams already in place. Ask the teams to design a life-size scarecrow with their own special theme to display in the office. They can use anything they like to build their scarecrow that they wish to bring in from home. Allow 2 weeks for the building of the scarecrows and another 2 weeks for the display.

One bank had 20 scarecrows in its call center, each with a different theme, including:
• Scarlet O'Scarecrow
• Priscilla, Queen of the Scarecrows
• The Wicked Scarecrow of the West
• Scarecrow of the Opera
• The Working Girl Scarecrow
• Three Heads are Better Than One Crow

At the end of the month, invite an executive to visit the office to select the first, second and third prize winners.

PRIZE Give cash prizes of about $100, $60 and $40 to the winning teams to spend any way they want.

BENEFIT • Helps stimulate positive energy instead of negative energy
• Gives people fond memories of their office
• Causes lots of laughter as each team's sense of humor is displayed through its scarecrow

SOURCE Jeannine Walsh

WE ARE HAVING A

SCARE-CROW COMPETITION

Your team is invited to participate by designing a
life-size scarecrow with your own special theme to
display in your team area.

You have just 2 weeks to put your scarecrow together!

First, second and third prize winners will be

announced on _____

The Hot House Room

In any company where staff deal with the stress and repetition of high customer contact, they need an outlet to let off steam.

PURPOSE • To reduce stress

GROUP SIZE Any amount of people

RESOURCE A room or section in the office, paint and decorations, and basic stress-free items such as beanbags or a punching bag

METHOD Provide a room or section in the office where people can go to let off steam. Ask staff what they would like the room to look like, then invite everyone who wants to be involved to plan, paint and decorate the room. As a guideline, suggest that the room should not look anything like an office and appeal as much as possible to the imagination of staff members.

Once the room is finished, assign a team to be responsible for the room each month. Suggest that, during the time that it is in charge of the room, each team brings in magazines, cartoon books, posters, toys, games or stress-relieving items. At the end of the month, the team should remove its contribution, so that the next team can start afresh.

Every 6 months, provide a prize for the team that does the best job managing the Hot House Room.

PRIZE Breakfast for the team at a nearby restaurant

BENEFIT • Gets staff involved in handling their stress in a productive manner
• Keeps the room fresh and exciting each month

SOURCE Carolyn Greenwich

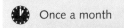

The Gossip Columnist

Many office workers are determined to gossip about their peers. This can create animosity and disenchantment among staff. One way to deal with gossip is to make fun of it.

PURPOSE
- To give people something to gossip about that is harmless and fun

GROUP SIZE 10 to 15 people

RESOURCE Copies of gossip magazines for prizes

METHOD Each month, ask one staff member to be the gossip columnist for the month. Their job is to collect information about each person in the team. Names are changed to protect the innocent, so their first job is to ask each person to provide a fictitious name that they wish to go by for the month. Each gossip columnist will need to come up with 3 headlines for their gossip newsletter, such as: 'My Deep Dark Secret', 'My Most Embarrassing Moment', 'True Confessions' or 'My Fantasy'. During the month, the gossip columnist asks each person in the team for information that is either true, true in part or absolutely false in each of these 3 areas.

The gossip columnist then publishes their 'gossip rag' at the end of the month. Everyone is given a chance to guess the identities of the people in the stories, based on the information that they have read. The person who gets the most right wins the prize.

PRIZE A copy of a gossip magazine

BENEFIT
- Gives everyone something to look forward to
- Causes laughter and fun in the office

SOURCE Carolyn Greenwich

Monthly Theme Day

Staff at one travel and tour company had so much fun with theme days that they decided to make them a monthly event for a day each month.

PURPOSE
• To lift morale and give everyone something to look forward to each month

GROUP SIZE
20 or more people—the more people you have, the better

RESOURCE
Small prizes (the food, decorations and costumes are supplied by the staff)

METHOD
Each month, give a different department or team the responsibility of organizing a theme day. The team selects the theme and sends out invitations to each individual in the company who will be participating. On the invitation, the team members should suggest what they would like everyone to wear or bring to work for the day. For example, if the theme is 'A Teddy Bear's Picnic', they may ask everyone to bring in their favorite cuddly toy. If the theme for the day is 'Red', they may ask everyone to dress in red or decorate their desks in red.

The invitations should list the prizes for the best dressed person, the best desk decoration or the best symbol of the theme day brought to work, and include what food items everyone should bring for the potluck lunch. The food selection should be in keeping with the theme day, so for a teddy bear's picnic, for example, each person would be assigned to bring a different item of picnic food.

Announce the prize winners at the lunch and award the prizes.

PRIZE
Select prizes that are symbolic of the theme for the day. For example, for a teddy bear's picnic, the winners might be given a box of teddy bear cookies.

BENEFIT
• A great team-building activity, because it gives every team or department an opportunity to plan an event
• A guaranteed morale-booster

SOURCE
Susie James Brown

Murder

An hilarious time was created when one team leader decided to create this simple game called 'Murder'. Team members were immediately energized and put into terrific spirits.

PURPOSE • To create fun and laughter in the office

GROUP SIZE 10 to 20 people

METHOD The objective of this game is to be the last person left alive according to the rules of the game.

Put the names of all the staff who are playing the game into a hat. Each person playing the game picks out a name and keeps this name secret. This is the name of the person that they will try to murder simply by touching them and saying 'You're murdered'. For a person to be murdered, they must be alone in a room or out of eyesight of anyone else when they are touched. This may require creative ways to lure the intended victim into the photocopy room or lunch room when no one else is present.

The murdered person is then out of the game and they pass on the name of the person that they are trying to murder to the person who has just murdered them.

The last person left alive is the winner.

PRIZE Because the winner has 'murdered' the most people, the prize is a certificate of commitment (see page 30) and the assignment of a task that is very unpopular. Naturally, this prize is kept secret or no one would try to win the game!

BENEFIT • Sends your team the message that having fun is part of the office philosophy

SOURCE Craig Horley

29

This is to certify that

_____

has won the game of

MURDER

To do penance for this,
you have been given
the task of

_____

_____

_____

_____

_____

Signed _____

Loaded Treasure

This is a quick energy booster that promotes fun in the office on days when everyone is overworked and only focused on getting the job done. Instead of staff resenting being overworked, this activity provides a way to reduce stress and show appreciation.

PURPOSE
- To boost enthusiasm, maintain morale and have fun

GROUP SIZE
15 to 75 people

RESOURCE
A treasure chest or box decorated to look like a treasure chest and small goodies for the treasure chest

METHOD
Fill the treasure chest with the goodies, such as mini candy bars, packets of chips, stress balls, novelty pens and other novelty items that staff will enjoy.

Twice during the day ask a manager or team leader to walk around the office and give every team member their choice of goodies from the treasure chest.

At the end of the day, select winners from a number of categories such as:
1. most stressed out
2. most calm
3. top performer in the category/ies of your choice
4. most enthusiastic
5. most helpful

Let the winners select additional prizes from the treasure chest in turn until all the prizes are gone.

REWARD
Instant recognition for everyone in the office for working under pressure on a particularly busy day

BENEFIT
- Energy levels rise when staff are recognized by the gesture of taking goodies from the treasure chest
- Helps everyone feel good and keeps people from becoming upset with each other in busy times

SOURCE
Brenda Shields

Coffee Break Quiz

Lots of people like trivia quizzes and they are a fun way to enjoy morning and afternoon tea breaks. This easy activity can be done for just fun or as a way to increase staff knowledge of products or services within the organization.

PURPOSE • To have fun and to reinforce product and service knowledge

GROUP SIZE 10 to 200

RESOURCE A box with a slot in it for the completed quizzes and paper for photocopying the quizzes

METHOD On a weekly basis, assign a pair or team to write a quiz on popular culture based on television shows, current events, movies and music, as well as company information such as products and services and new industry developments.

Use the quiz provided (see page 33) to get started and then use the following guidelines for writing future quizzes:
1. Provide 20 multiple choice questions.
2. Include a range of easy to more difficult questions.
3. Of the 20 questions, 15 should cover general themes such as music, television shows, movies or current events, and 5 should pertain to the business or organization.

Once you have approved a quiz, it should be photocopied and put in the staff room. Any member of staff who wishes to complete the quiz can do so at any coffee break during the first four days of the week. They can get help on the answers from others or they can complete the quiz on their own. This will increase participation. When staff have finished the quiz, they write their name at the top and put the completed quiz in the Coffee Break Quiz box.

On the fifth day, draw a quiz out of the box. The first correctly answered quiz to be drawn wins the weekly prize.

PRIZE A different prize each week to the value of $10—the prize is selected by the pair or team that writes the quiz.

SOURCE Alex Greenwich and Carolyn Greenwich

1. On which TV soap will you find the Foresters and the Spectras?
   (a) 'Days of Our Lives'
   (b) 'The Young and the Restless'
   (c) 'The Bold and the Beautiful'
   (d) 'General Hospital'

2. Who was Australia's first prime minister?
   (a) Barton
   (b) Cook
   (c) McMahon
   (d) Fraser

3. Which former American president and vice-president was never elected to either position?
   (a) Carter
   (b) Ford
   (c) Bush
   (d) Nixon

4. What was the name of J.R. Ewing's wife on 'Dallas'?
   (a) Crystal
   (b) Alexis
   (c) Pamela
   (d) Sue Ellen

5. Which country shares borders with both France and Spain?
   (a) Portugal
   (b) Andorra
   (c) Luxembourg
   (d) Liechtenstein

6. What is the name of Al Gore's wife?
   (a) Rose
   (b) Tipper
   (c) Hillary
   (d) Susan

7. On which TV show did all the actresses receive an Emmy for Best Actress?
   (a) 'Dallas'
   (b) 'Designing Women'
   (c) 'The Golden Girls'
   (d) 'Sisters'

8. What is the address of the famous 'Melrose Place' apartment complex?
   (a) 6868
   (b) 4616
   (c) 5782
   (d) 1122

9. Which country has won the last two America's Cups?
   (a) Italy
   (b) Australia
   (c) USA
   (d) New Zealand

10. Where was Mel Gibson born?
    (a) Australia
    (b) USA
    (c) New Zealand
    (d) England

11. What is the capital of Spain?
    (a) Barcelona
    (b) Madrid
    (c) Majorca
    (d) Lisbon

12. Where does billionaire Bill Gates live?
    (a) Beverly Hills
    (b) New York
    (c) Seattle
    (d) Silicon Valley

13. Who played Norm on 'Cheers'?
    (a) Tony Danza
    (b) Woody Harrelson
    (c) Kelsey Grammer
    (d) George Wendt

14. What is the capital of New Zealand?
    (a) Auckland
    (b) Wellington
    (c) Christchurch
    (d) Gisborne

15. What was the title of Carolyn Greenwich's first book?
    (a) *The Fun Factory*
    (b) *Fun at Work*
    (c) *The Fun Factor*
    (d) *Work Place Games*

Answers: c, a, b, d, b, b, c, b, d, b, b, c, d, b, c

The Calorie Club

Everyone has goals outside the workplace that they are trying to achieve. Losing weight and eating a more healthy diet are goals that many people share. By joining forces to reach individual goals, colleagues can help and support each other.

PURPOSE
- To help people at work who are interested in losing weight to help each other

GROUP SIZE 5 to 20 people per club

RESOURCE Scales, a weight log and a room to use each week

METHOD Establish your Calorie Club by inviting interested parties to the first meeting, either by word of mouth or by invitation. Once the club has started, anyone can join at any time.

The purpose of the club is to help people to stay focused on their weight loss goals. Everyone follows their own diet and sets their own goals. No one reveals their weight to anyone else. The club meets once a week for half an hour. It costs $2 to attend the meeting. People weigh themselves and write down how much they have lost or gained in the weight log. If they have gained weight, they pay $5. The weigh-in works on an honor system, so that no one is put in the position of having to reveal their weight at any time.

At each meeting, the group may decide to set aside 5 to 10 minutes to allow members to talk about recipes or health tips that they wish to share.

The club needs to be driven and organized by someone. Once a month ask a different member to take on the responsibility of organizing the meetings for that month.

After the initial expenses of paying for the scales and the weight log, the money collected is given to charity. The club decides which charity to support each quarter.

BENEFIT
- The self-satisfaction of helping others as well as oneself
- Giving to charity
- Saves time and money by not attending commercial weight loss centers

SOURCE Jeannine Walsh

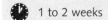

Don't Lose Your Marbles

In times of stress people sometimes feel that they are going to 'lose their marbles' because of the extra pressure. To make light of a stressful situation and to help people stay focused, here is an easy, visual game.

PURPOSE • To help staff to stay positive and reduce negative attitudes or behaviors

GROUP SIZE Works best in a team of 4 to 12 people

RESOURCE Lots of colorful marbles and an attractive jar with a lid for each staff member

METHOD Give everyone in the team a jar with 10 marbles inside. Explain that the objective of the game is to win as many marbles as possible during the duration of the game, as well as to avoid losing the marbles that they have or have earned. Explain the various ways that they can win or lose marbles. For example,

To win one marble they need to:

1. pay someone a compliment or show appreciation at least three times in one day
2. reach the daily productivity target (one marble for each daily goal reached)
3. win the 'Marvel of the Day' award for the most positive, helpful attitude, as awarded by the team leader (see page 37)
4. win the random marble draw at the end of the day

To lose one marble they need to:

1. make an error
2. have a negative attitude or use negative language
3. be late for work or arrive late back from lunch
   At the end of each day, award/deduct marbles as appropriate. The person who has collected the most marbles at the end of the competition is the winner.

PRIZE First place redeems their marbles for $1.00 each; second place redeems their marbles for 50 cents each and third place redeems their marbles for 25 cents each. Each winner is given a 'Marvel of the Team' certificate (see page 37).

BENEFIT
- A fun, visual competition that is easy to do
- Helps to reinforce behavior that leads to higher productivity
- Helps reduce tardiness

SOURCE Victor Greenwich Jr

MARVEL OF THE DAY

Name _____

MARVEL OF THE TEAM

Name _____

Winning Attitudes

Nearly every company has a vision and mission statement that is put in place to help people stay focused on the big picture. Winning attitudes in business are those attitudes that people are encouraged to develop and maintain to achieve the big picture. This activity will help determine what winning attitudes are important to your company and will bring excellent results in adopting these attitudes.

PURPOSE
• To establish 5 winning attitudes that all staff will be encouraged to demonstrate on a consistent basis

GROUP SIZE
Any number

RESOURCE
Poster paper, paint, felt pens and any decorative materials used to create winning attitude posters or decorations

METHOD
Hold team meetings and ask each team to come up with 5 winning attitudes that they feel are in line with the vision and mission statement of the department or organization. Further explain that these 5 attitudes should also help create a positive and productive work culture and create a happy, results-oriented environment. The attitudes are described by a few words or simple phrases, such as:
1. optimistic
2. results-focused
3. get it right the first time
4. helpful
5. understanding

Once each team has come up with 5 winning attitudes, write all the attitudes submitted onto a voting paper and ask each person in the organization to choose the 5 attitudes that they would most like to see demonstrated on a regular basis in the office, call center or organization.

When the 5 attitudes have been agreed on by popular vote, divide the organization, office or call center into 5 winning attitude teams. Give each team a different attitude, and for the next 5 weeks, each team takes it in turns to help everyone in the organization to focus on its particular attitude. The teams can decorate the office with their winning attitudes and reinforce their attitude in any way they would like. For example, they may choose to:

1. hold a theme day
2. create and distribute small A4 posters showing their winning attitude for people to display at their desks
3. put on a morning tea, and give a talk or act out a play that demonstrates why their winning attitude is so important
4. create a weekly competition that focuses on their 'winning attitude'

At the end of the 5 weeks, host a morning tea to congratulate everyone on their involvement, effort and enthusiasm. Announce the 5 winners of the Winning Attitudes Awards to help people stay focused on developing and maintaining the winning attitudes. Each quarter, people are nominated by their peers for demonstrating excellence in one of the winning attitudes that is now a part of the company culture. The 5 winners are selected by popular vote or by a panel of their peers.

PRIZE Winning Attitudes Award (see page 40) and invitation to the Winning Attitudes Lunch

SOURCE Victor Greenwich and Carolyn Greenwich

Winning Attitudes Award

Name _____

Demonstrating
excellence in _____

_____

_____

_____

2 REINFORCING
PROFESSIONALISM

A clever manager is always looking for ways to reinforce and improve the level of professionalism in the office. This means developing leadership skills and getting staff involved in looking for ways to improve work. It also means rewarding professional behavior and letting people know in a fun way what behaviors are not acceptable. Here are a number of workplace activities and games that some managers have found to be extremely effective.

Rotating Jobs

Rotating the jobs in the office helps staff to avoid burnout from repetitive tasks and keeps them in the job longer. It simply requires a little thought and organisation to give structure to a number of distinct functions, which staff rotate over a 3- to 6-month period. Rotating jobs also helps develop staff members, as they learn new skills.

PURPOSE
• To uphold staff members' interest and enthusiasm for their work by continually providing new challenges and different tasks

GROUP SIZE
5 to 50 people

RESOURCE
A chart of the responsibilities for each function that is to be rotated and a roster of the staff who will be rotating positions

METHOD
Look at the various functions or jobs that need to be done in your office and that can be rotated easily. You may look at rotating certain tasks or whole responsibilities. For example, in a customer service and sales call center, these functions may include:
1. participation in any outbound telesales campaigns
2. involvement in more specialist activities such as debt collection
3. involvement in more complex technical or billing call management
4. implementation of a 'liaison' role, where customer service phone representatives each own a 'portfolio', such as marketing or recruitment, or a certain geographical territory
5. participation in special projects

It is important to keep salaries at the same level, so that staff will be less inclined to hang on to the various functions purely for monetary reward and to see themselves as superior to colleagues in the short term.

REWARD
Certificate of accomplishment (see page 44)

BENEFIT   • Staff have a greater understanding and appreciation of the business
           • Staff become multiskilled and more valuable to the business
           • Staff become more professional as they grow in their skills and knowledge

SOURCE   John Barry

Name _____

Certificate
of Accomplishment
for being multi-skilled in

1. _____

2. _____

3. _____

Signed _____

I'm Here to Work

A customer service center in a bank with a high number of temporary staff found that the 'temp attitude' was affecting the professionalism of the other staff. The temps were hired to help out in busy times, but these would fluctuate throughout the day, and during the slower times the temps would chat, distract the others in the office and generally bring down the standard of professionalism in the office. This activity changed all that and created resources for training and reference for all staff.

PURPOSE
- To use slow times to build knowledge and keep people focused on their responsibilities

GROUP SIZE   Any number of people

RESOURCE   Folder and paper

METHOD   Give each temp a folder containing some sample questions and a brief to investigate a topic, product, procedure or some competitor information. Give them a time frame and a broad outline of where to look for the information.

During slow periods, ask the temps to work on their projects. They can photocopy any area of relevant manuals or brochures that will provide this information and should highlight all the information that is most important.

Each person's folder is reviewed by the team leader when it is finished. It may be returned if more information is required to complete the project satisfactorily.

BENEFIT
- Keeps everyone focused and allows some of the brighter staff to be creative and very thorough. At the bank, staff were amazed at how much information was found on subjects that was not previously known or apparent. The folders became resources for training and references for all staff to use.
- At the bank, the project worked so well that it was also used for permanent staff in slower periods. It made people act with the professional attitude 'I'm here to work'.

SOURCE   Barbara Kernos

45

Leaders in Waiting

In order to help staff to prepare for advancement, and keep them involved and enthusiastic while they wait for an opportunity for promotion, it helps to establish a 'Leaders in Waiting' program. This program is ideally suited to a call center, but it can be adapted for any type of situation.

PURPOSE • To train and retain people with leadership potential

GROUP SIZE 1 to 10 people, depending on the number of opportunities within the company

RESOURCE Clearly defined leadership standards

METHOD Inform all staff of the selection process and the standard of skills, knowledge and experience necessary to become a team leader. Let staff know that, while there may be only one position available, those who miss the promotion this time can become 'Leaders in Waiting'. They will be called on to handle special leadership activities from time to time, such as:
1. acting as relief team leader when the team leader is away for short periods
2. preparing reports or administration activities to take the load off the team leader
3. managing casual or temporary staff
4. coaching and training staff in their specific areas of expertise

REWARD The new skills and experience that the 'Leaders in Waiting' gain; 'Leader in Waiting' certificate (see page 47)

BENEFIT • When the next team leader role is available, the 'Leaders in Waiting' can be assessed for the position based on how they performed in their leadership activities
• The company ensures that it has trained people in place to take on leadership roles when sudden vacancies arise

SOURCE John Barry

LEADER
IN WAITING

Name _____

Professional Potential

What happens when it appears that a staff member has the intelligence and ability to act in a professional manner, but they are not living up to their potential? Kris Cole, author of *Crystal Clear Communication*, suggests the following method as a means of understanding the underlying problem and taking steps to help the staff member to realise their professional potential.

PURPOSE
: • To help an unprofessional staff member to become more valuable to the company and themselves

GROUP SIZE
: One-on-one conversation between the staff member and their manager

METHOD
: First, the manager must answer the following questions:

1. Does the employee understand clearly what is expected of them and how they contribute to the department or the company as a whole?
2. Could the employee do the job well if their life depended on it?
3. Is anything stopping the employee from doing the job well, such as a lack of time or information, cumbersome or sloppy procedures, or outdated technology?
4. As a manager, am I setting a good example?

Next, the manager should ask the employee the following questions:

1. Has management clearly outlined to you what the expectations of your job are? Has management clarified how you contribute to the company as a whole when you perform your job?
2. If your life depended on it, is there any aspect of your job that you could not perform well?
3. Are there any obstacles at work stopping you from doing your job well?
4. As your manager, is there anything that I can do to help you become more professional in your position?

Using the assessments of the situation from the perceptions of both the manager and the employee, the following plan of action will help the employee to realize their professional potential:

1. If both parties answer 'No' to the first question, then the manager and employee should sit down and have a chat. The manager should explain clearly to the staff member how doing their job well contributes to the whole department or organization. The manager should quantify the company's expectations and establish time frames for meeting them.

2. If the manager answers 'Yes' to the second question, this suggests the problem is a motivational one, while 'No' could mean that the employee is in the wrong job or needs more training.

3. If both parties answer 'Yes' to the third question, then the manager will have to take a serious look at staffing levels, systems and procedures, and support mechanisms such as technology.

4. If the manager answers 'No' to the fourth question and the employee answers 'Yes', this suggests that the manager may need some leadership and management training.

REWARD New confidence and professionalism for the staff member

BENEFIT • Helps the manager to assess the problems clearly and concentrate on the solution(s) that will bring the best results

SOURCE Kris Cole

Knowledge Pursuit

To help staff members maintain their level of professionalism it is important that their level of product or service knowledge is always up to date. Learning becomes easy when you make a game of it. Almost any board game can be adapted for this purpose, or you can create your own board game.

PURPOSE
• To update staff with new product knowledge

GROUP SIZE
3 to 4 people per team; 4 to 5 teams

RESOURCE
Board game, counters and die, questions and answers

METHOD
1. Divide the participants into teams, taking into account the level of knowledge of the players so that the teams are fairly evenly matched.
2. Each team has to answer a question in turn. A team member roles the die and the facilitator asks the team a product or service knowledge question. If the answer is correct, the team moves forward and another member roles the die again for a second question. If the team gives an incorrect answer, or answers 2 questions correctly, the facilitator then asks the next team a question.
3. The game is completed when one team reaches the finish line.

PRIZE
The fun of competition

BENEFIT
• Enables staff to develop and enhance their product knowledge by answering specific product and service-related questions
• Promotes teamwork by encouraging the team to agree on an answer
• Helps the facilitator identify areas of strengths and weaknesses

SOURCE
Craig MacDonald

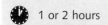

WISE Leadership

All leaders want to appear wise in the eyes of their team. What does it mean to be wise in the eyes of those that you lead? What practical ways can you demonstrate your wisdom? This activity can help you to become a more effective leader and get results.

PURPOSE
• To help leaders get a better understanding of what people really look for in a leader

GROUP SIZE
4 to 5 people per discussion group

METHOD
Wise leaders know that the best way to lead and manage a team is to determine what motivates people and act on that. To help leaders in the organization understand the motivation of their team members, the acronym WISE is used for the 4 areas of motivation.

W   What is in it for me?
I   Involvement
S   Simplify
E   Energize

For each of these categories, ask the teams to discuss ways to get the best out of each team and each team member. A handout is provided (see page 53) with some of the questions to ask and answer for each category, including:

What is in it for me?

1. Why do team members perform well?
2. What do they need from their leader to feel valued?
3. What does the leader need to do to retain good staff?

Involvement

1. What action(s) will involve staff in the big picture?
2. What involvement will gain their commitment to excellence?
3. How can the most apathetic staff members become involved?

Simplify

1. What are the easiest ways to get the best out of team members?
2. How can leaders take away the frustrations, stress and hassles that affect team members while they are trying to do their job?
3. How can management simplify processes and procedures to achieve a better outcome?

Energize

1. How can leaders stimulate positive attitudes?
2. What can leaders do to create fun and happiness in the office?
3. How can leaders energize the office on a continual basis?

Provide each team with a copy of the handout to record their answers.

Following the discussion on WISE leadership, the next step is to determine what to implement and how to implement it.

BENEFIT
- Gives leaders a clear understanding of what people expect of them
- Turns theory into practical actions

SOURCE Carolyn Greenwich

WHAT IS IN IT FOR ME?

1. Why do team members perform well?
2. What do they need from their leader to feel valued?
3. What does the leader need to do to retain good staff?

INVOLVEMENT

1. What action(s) will involve staff in the big picture?
2. What involvement will gain their commitment to excellence?
3. How can the most apathetic staff members become involved?

SIMPLIFY

1. What are the easiest ways to get the best out of team members?
2. How can leaders take away the frustrations, stress and hassles that affect team members while they are trying to do their job?
3. How can management simplify processes and procedures to achieve a better outcome?

ENERGIZE

1. How can leaders stimulate positive attitudes?
2. What can leaders do to create fun and happiness in the office?
3. How can leaders energize the office on a continual basis?

The Late Lotto

A few staff coming in 5 to 10 minutes late each day can be a costly exercise for a business if left unchecked. Here is a simply strategy that worked wonders for a marketing company.

PURPOSE
- To ensure that all staff are at their desks ready to start work at the designated start time

GROUP SIZE Any number

RESOURCE A piggy bank

METHOD First, make sure that all staff know what it means to be on time. Does 'on time' mean that they walk through the door at that time and then get themselves ready? Or does it mean that they are at their desks ready to start work? In some offices, such as call centers, this is very easy to monitor, because it means that staff are logged on the phone at the starting time ready to start work.

Let everyone know that, when they are late, they will be asked to put 50 cents into the late lotto piggy bank. It is up to all staff to ensure that any late starters make their donation of 50 cents into the late lotto piggy bank. No excuses are accepted.

PRIZE When enough money is collected, purchase a lotto ticket for the whole office.

BENEFIT
- It becomes impossible for staff to slide into work 5 to 10 minutes late without anyone noticing. As a consequence, staff start arriving on time.

SOURCE Judy Purdon

5 weeks

Self-Managed Work Teams

Self-managed work teams are teams that divide up the responsibilities of the team leader among the team members. Giving the team members the responsibility of managing their team has many benefits for the company, the team members and the customers.

PURPOSE
- To help people to learn new skills while on-the-job and to expand the capability of the team

GROUP SIZE 5 to 12 people

RESOURCE Butcher's paper and felt pens

METHOD Communicate to team members the benefits of self-managed work teams for the company, the team members and the customers that they are serving. Discuss the team members' issues and concerns and encourage their participation.

As a group, ask them to identify a typical team leader's responsibilities or tasks, and then ask them what competencies they feel are needed to successfully take on those responsibilities. Ask each team member to nominate 2 or 3 responsibilities or tasks that they are interested in and feel competent to perform. Then narrow it down to 1 task for each person interested in participating in the self-managed work team. To be successful, all members in the team must agree to participate.

The next day, meet with each individual to discuss the process(es) associated with their responsibility or task. Be available on an ongoing basis to answer any questions or queries that they may have as they occur. Arrange meetings at scheduled times to review work undertaken and discuss any new concerns.

At the end of 4 to 5 weeks, gather the team together and change each person's responsibilities or tasks. The person who has done the job previously is now in the position to help the new person perform their particular team leader's task.

BENEFIT   • Involvement equals ownership
          • Helps people to learn new skills
          • Helps keep staff interested and motivated

SOURCE   Margaret Casey

1 month

Cutting Through the Paperwork

Administration staff are sometimes left out of the fun and games that are used in sales and customer service environments. Improving the work flow and creating a bit of fun does not take much time and is greatly appreciated by staff.

PURPOSE
• To ensure that staff work well together, meet deadlines and are flexible in working with others in the team to accomplish a team goal

GROUP SIZE
5 to 10 people

RESOURCE
Whiteboard and pens

METHOD
Create a large chart for all to see on the whiteboard. Identify the team goals through discussion. Clearly mark the team goal for the work to be completed by the end of the week. Each day, mark what the team has achieved for the day, and make a note of individual totals as well.

To add variety and encourage teamwork, roster a different person each day to be in charge of organizing the team. It becomes their duty to:
1. allocate work for the day, and encourage and support others
2. collect daily work sheets and calculate the work completed by the team and individual members
3. record progress for the day on the chart

BENEFIT
• Creates more pride in being part of a team and achieving results together
• Places a focus on meeting and exceeding goals and deadlines

SOURCE
Lyn Prince

Shooting Stars

To encourage ongoing professional behavior, one teleservices company put into place a loyalty program, similar to loyalty programs found in the marketplace. By rewarding staff for professional behavior, this initiative was a huge success.

PURPOSE
- To put into place a loyalty program that encourages professional behavior through reward points called 'Stars'

GROUP SIZE Any number of staff

RESOURCE Star cut-outs (see page 60) and star mobiles hanging from the ceiling as a visual reinforcement of the loyalty program, and star-shaped posters of the prizes hung on the wall

METHOD Develop a loyalty program with basic terms and conditions that can be easily understood by all. Assign certain behaviors or accomplishments a star value. Some star awards may be accomplished by meeting specific targets and others may be awarded through management's judgment. Decide what professional behavior you wish to encourage. For example, you may award stars in some of the following areas:
1. no sick days in a 2-month period
2. 100% accuracy over a monthly period
3. reaching specific targets
4. excellent customer feedback
5. volunteering for and completing a special project
6. excellent rating in a call monitoring session
7. positive attitude in a difficult situation
8. performance above the call of duty
9. resolving a difficult customer complaint situation

Provide all staff members with their own 'Shooting Star' loyalty program book, which outlines the terms and conditions of the program. Each time staff are awarded stars, provide stars to put in the book.

At certain times of the year, such as Christmas, St Valentine's Day, Easter, Hallowe'en or other holidays, offer opportunities to cash in stars for prizes. Let staff know in advance what the prizes are, so that they can start working towards their goal.

You will need to keep your own spreadsheet of all stars given and redeemed. When you wish to finish the activity, let people know 3 months in advance, so that they can work towards the last opportunity to redeem their stars.

PRIZE Ask staff what they would like in the way of larger prizes within a certain price limit. Also include smaller prizes such as pens, boxes of chocolates and movie tickets, which can be redeemed for just one or two stars. This will help people to use up their extra stars after they have redeemed a larger prize.

BENEFIT
- Morale remains high because the recognition is constant
- People feel special when rewarded stars
- Staff focus on what is important to management

SOURCE Brenda Shields

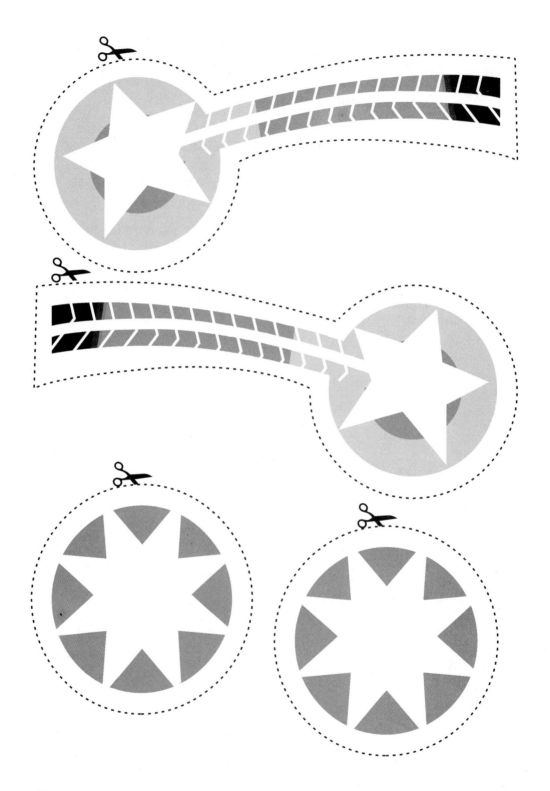

Check You Out Program

One international shipping company organized a unique way for managers to recognize and encourage professional behavior within their departments, by creating check books of certificates worth various dollar values for managers to reward staff. Each year, new improvements are made to the program at the suggestion of staff and management.

PURPOSE
• To help people to focus on professional behavior as defined by management and emulated by others in the organization

GROUP SIZE
10 to 1000 people

RESOURCE
'Check You Out' check books (see page 63)

METHOD
Each year, the management team designs a check book that explains the professional behaviors that are to be encouraged and recognized that year. A theme should be chosen for the checks, such as 'Mission Possible', and this should appear at the top of each check. Each check should describe the behavior being rewarded (see page 63). The behavior might be:

1. 'Let's work together', to reward team work
2. 'Make every day count', for consistent efficiency
3. 'Be an agent of change', for an individual who embraces change
4. 'Assume a winning attitude', for being a positive role model
5. 'It's not just a job, it's a mission', for results-oriented action and achievement

Each manager is given a check book with 50 checks and a budget for the year, depending on the size of the department. The manager, or any person in the department with the manager's authority, can fill out a check in the check book any time they wish to acknowledge a positive behavior. The manager has to sign each check and this is then presented to the person being rewarded. At the same time, the manager presents a small gift purchased from the budget.

PRIZE The recognition of management or peers in the form of a check certificate; movie tickets, chocolates, gift vouchers, etc.

BENEFIT • Lets staff know exactly what behaviors are appreciated within the company
• Helps bring the company mission statement alive
• Gives staff a means to reward and appreciate their peers

SOURCE Hamish Bamford

'CHECK YOU OUT' CHECK

Date _____

Made to the order of _____

For demonstrating _____

By _____

We would like to reward you with _____

_____

Signed _____

Sacred Cows

At times of great change, new initiatives can threaten the confidence levels of staff. A great way to prevent this is to get people in the organization involved in creating the new initiatives to cope with such change. In the call center of one leading bank, staff were encouraged to identify the 'Sacred Cows' within their center. A sacred cow is a procedure, policy or process that is no longer relevant or effective and no longer meets the goals and values of the business. This bank made 43 improvements in 11 months based on the 'Sacred Cow' program.

PURPOSE
• To have staff identify procedures, policies and processes that are outdated and to get them to suggest improvements

GROUP SIZE
Encourage everyone in the call center, division or organization to become involved

RESOURCE
Lots of cut-outs of cows hanging from the ceilings (see page 68), and pictures of cows and toy cows displayed around the office

METHOD
Hold team meetings to launch the Sacred Cow program. Start by giving the definition of a sacred cow as 'a time-consuming, inefficient or outdated process or procedure'. To further identify a sacred cow, explain that it:
1. is something that frustrates you
2. costs unnecessary money
3. reduces service levels
4. negatively affects morale
5. maintains the status quo
6. costs time
7. suppresses creativity

Explain that this is a program that each person can contribute to. As an individual or as a team, staff will have the opportunity to identify sacred cows and suggest new, improved processes or procedures. They will be rewarded for the ideas that are implemented and result in cost savings, revenue gains and ease of operations.

Give clear outlines as to the manner in which the program is to be run. Explain what is expected, how participants will be supported and the role of management. Have tools available to everyone such as:

1. a simple form for ideas
2. a process to review ideas
3. a central register for ideas
4. a record of the status of ideas (proceeding, declined, implemented)
5. a record of the assessment of the value or cost saving of each idea

As an improvement is being developed, let staff know that management will help by:

1. giving an assessment of the impact of the policy, system or product
2. helping get the 'right' people involved to develop and implement the procedure
3. allocating time and resources for implementing the improvement
4. monitoring progress
5. using their contacts within the organization to obtain support and remove barriers
6. giving feedback

Once the improvement is accepted it will go through a process that will involve:

1. communicating the new procedure or process to all parties involved
2. running a pilot of the new procedure or process
3. training staff in the new procedure or process
4. changing handbooks and curricula to reflect the new procedure or process
5. evaluating the new procedure or process
6. modifying the new procedure or process

REWARD Award trophies to those staff members whose ideas for new improvements are implemented and successful. Have a 'Sacred Cow' honor role (see page 67) with the names of all contributors.

BENEFIT • Utilizes the talent, energy and ideas of everyone in the organization
• Gives people a meaningful way to be recognized
• Helps people to become ready for change and embrace change

SOURCE Carolyn Adams, David Johnson, Paula Luethen, Ann–Marie Catlin and Kate McKechnie. The idea was adapted from *Sacred Cows Make the Best Burgers* by Robert Kriegel and David Brandt.

MOO-VERS AND SHAKERS

YOU ARE NOW PART
OF THE HONOR ROLE
FOR YOUR GREAT IDEA

Tea Tags

In a customer service environment, not everyone can dash off to morning or afternoon tea at the same time. If some people are late back or others go early, then suddenly those who are left can become easily annoyed. A customer service phone center devised this method to keep everyone punctual and happy.

PURPOSE
- To ensure that staff members do not get annoyed with each other by overstaying their tea breaks by providing a simple visual system that tracks the number of people away from their desks

GROUP SIZE 10 to 20 people

RESOURCE A board and some material to make tea tags (see page 70)

METHOD
1. Ensure that everyone knows exactly when and how long they are scheduled to have their tea breaks.
2. Place the board up high so that everyone can see it from their workstation.
3. Make some tags and hang on the board the number of tags that indicates the number of people that are allowed to be away on a tea break at any one time. When staff go on their break, they take a tag off the board to indicate that they are on break. When they come back from their break, they hang the tag back on the board. If there are no tags on the board, no more staff members are allowed to go for a break—they have to wait for someone to return.

BENEFIT
- Provides better internal and external customer service
- Gives a clear signal of expectations

SOURCE Robyn Taylor

Office Mates

One of the easiest ways to ensure quick results in any behavior that you wish to improve is to pair up people of differing abilities, then simply create a competition with other pairs. New skills and abilities are quickly transferred from the strongest to the less experienced member of the team as the pair competes to win the competition.

PURPOSE
• To help transfer skills from the experienced to the less experienced, or the successful to the less successful

GROUP SIZE
6 to 18 people, working in pairs

RESOURCE
Whiteboard and pens

METHOD
Select the behavior that you wish the more experienced people in the team to share with the more inexperienced. It needs to be a skill that has an outcome that can be measured. Here are some examples:
1. cross-selling
2. selling
3. managing time effectively
4. controlling the duration of a call in a call center
5. generating work flows
6. resolving complaints

Team up the top performers with the less experienced or less able. Create a competition over a specified period of time. For example, you could hold the competition for a week, with the winner being the best performing pair. Or, if you wish to keep the competition going for a few weeks, you can pair up people with a new partner every week (and have a winning pair each week). This way, people have a chance to pass on their knowledge or to learn from more people.

PRIZE
Each week, award a prize of $25 to $50 in value for each member of the winning pair.

BENEFIT
• Improves knowledge within the team
• Stimulates productivity

SOURCE
Carolyn Greenwich

Critical Success Menu

The success of any organization depends on the continual development of its staff. Each person within the organization has certain basic skills that are critical to the successful outcome of their responsibilities. Many of these skills are very basic, but nonetheless vitally important. To help staff to focus on and improve these skills, develop and use a 'Critical Success Menu'.

PURPOSE • To build and develop skills and consistency of performance

GROUP SIZE Divide the organization into positions that are similar

METHOD Hold a meeting with each group that has similar responsibilities. In a customer service call center, each person is doing the same task, so the tasks should be broken down into 4 broad categories, such as communication skills, sales and service skills, success–related issues, and development and growth issues. At the meeting, ask the group to come up with the skills that they would like to focus on improving. At the end of the session, you may have a Critical Success Menu that looks something like this:

Critical Success Menu

1. COMMUNICATION SKILLS
Listening
Voice tone
Questioning
Rapport
Customer focus
Language
Call control

2. SALES AND SERVICE SKILLS
Needs analysis; gaining information
Product knowledge
Cross-selling
Handling objections
Closing

3. SUCCESS-RELATED ISSUES
Professional attitudes
Work habits and time management
Accuracy
Teamwork
Adaptability
Use of resources

4. DEVELOPMENT AND GROWTH ISSUES
Leadership skills
Training skills
Coaching skills
Monitoring skills

Once everyone has agreed on the Critical Success Menu, embark on a coaching program. Meet with each team member on a fortnightly or monthly basis to select the area or areas in the Critical Success Menu that they would like to focus on improving. The team members should be encouraged to come up with methods of learning that suit their particular learning styles. For example, they may choose from a range of learning methods such as:

1. buddying with another staff member
2. reading a book on the subject
3. listening to tapes or watching a video
4. trying out techniques suggested by experts in the field
5. posting visual prompts as reminders and reinforcements
6. attending a training session
7. drawing a diagram

When you meet with the team member, the purpose is to come to an agreement on the goal, the coaching period and the learning actions that they will take to improve the skills. To evaluate success, discuss how best to evaluate progress. The goal may be measured easily by the use of statistics, or it may need to be evaluated more subjectively, by opinion or perception. A coaching record will act as a useful record of these discussions (see page 74).

SOURCE   Carolyn Greenwich

Coaching Record

Name: Coach:

Position: Coaching period:

Coaching goal:

_____

Benefits

To team member:

To customer:

To organization:

_____

What actions will help me accomplish my goal?

_____

How can we measure my success over the period?

_____

Evaluation of progress

My evaluation:

Coach's evaluation:

_____

Team member's signature_____Date_____

Coach's signature_____Date_____

The Improvement Team

Helping staff to focus on and lift productivity is always an issue in call centers, retail outlets and administration offices, as well as in dedicated sales teams. One very successful method is to hand-pick an improvement team from the front-line staff to come up with ways to lift productivity.

PURPOSE
• To develop new 'how-to strategies' to improve productivity

GROUP SIZE
3 to 6 people is a good number (any smaller or larger and the decision-making process begins to deteriorate through too few or too many opinions)

METHOD
1. Hand-pick your improvement team and ensure that you have a mix of both high and low performers. This will ensure involvement and valuable contributions from all levels of experience and success.
2. Gather the team members together to tell them that you are giving them a clear mandate to raise productivity through any means possible to the company with the resources currently available. Ask them to recommend a plan of action. Let them know what the impact of costs and the returns of low, medium and high productivity mean to the company.
3. Volunteer to be their 'data sourcer' and give them all the information that they may need to form their recommendation.
4. Then leave the team members alone to develop their strategies and recommendation. They should meet for approximately 2 hours per week over the next 4 weeks. During this time, meet with them on a weekly basis to hear their progress reports and give feedback or guidance if they ask you for it. Encourage them to trial a few ideas during this time to see if their ideas are having a positive impact.
5. At the end of the 4 weeks, meet with the team to hear their formal presentation. Work with them on the implementation of their recommended strategies.

REWARD   Provide a certificate of achievement or a letter of thanks (see page 77).

BENEFIT   • Once the empowerment and responsibility have been accepted by the team members, results follow quickly. Funnily enough, the improvement team members also improve their own productivity in the process.

SOURCE   John Barry

Thank
you

_____

for

_____

_____

_____

You are a valued member
of the

IMPROVEMENT
TEAM

The Great Race

One team member wanted to turn daily benchmarks, statistics and quotas into something fun, as well as to create better results through friendly competition. He approached his team leader with the idea of 'The Great Race'. Once the idea was implemented it grew and became even more creative as the whole team looked for ways to make the game even more fun and more visual.

PURPOSE
- To show statistics visually in a fun and innovative way
- To help improve professionalism and productivity

GROUP SIZE 6 to 10 individuals, pairs or teams

RESOURCE Cardboard, whiteboard, markers, magnets or Blu-Tack and checkered flags

METHOD
1. Ask each team, pair or individual to choose their favorite 'dream' car. Draw a small picture of each car onto cardboard (or see page 80), cut them out and attach a magnet or some Blu-Tack to the back of each car.
2. On a large whiteboard draw in the main straight of a racetrack going upwards, as well as a pit lane, a grandstand and some ripple strips. Color it in and decorate it to create a visual impact.
3. Use the left side of the main straight to reflect the production amount that you are attempting to reach each day. In a customer service phone center it could reflect the number of calls per hour taken by each representative. In a retail outlet it could reflect the number of customers assisted or new accounts opened.
4. Draw a finish line at the point that each person, team or pair is expected to achieve for the day. Position the cars on the track at the starting point. If an individual player is on leave, their car goes into the pit.
5. Each day or week award the first, second and third place winners with a checkered flag numbered with 1, 2 or 3 to

place at their work station or locker. Each day or week, as new winners are announced, the flags are passed on to the next winners.

6. Send out a memo with each day or week's statistics in the style of a motor sport's commentary. For example: 'Welcome back to our coverage of 'The Great Race'! Out in first place is the Ferrari driven by Marco and it has just crossed the finish line with a top speed of 9.5 calls per hour! But wait! The Jaguar driven by Romona has slid off the track after colliding with Maureen's Mercedes and has dropped to fifth place!!'

REWARD   Recognition by way of displaying the flag and seeing their car in first, second or third place on the race board

BENEFIT   • Lifts the spirits and creates interest and awareness in a fun way of everyone's productivity levels
          • As no prizes are awarded, it keeps the competition friendly
          • An inexpensive way to achieve great results

SOURCE   Mark Pugliese

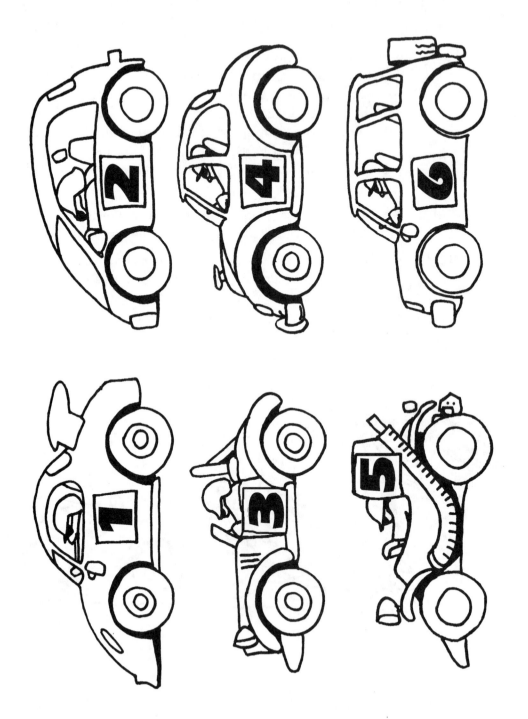

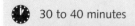

You Make the Difference

A manager wanted to help people to understand the importance of providing a higher level of customer service. In order to achieve this, he presented them with the following hypothetical situation.

PURPOSE • To improve staff members' professionalism by having them think of themselves as shareholders of a company

GROUP SIZE 10 to 20 people

RESOURCE Whiteboard and pens

METHOD At a meeting, present this hypothetical situation to the staff: Tell each one of them that they have just won $2 million in the lotto. They have quit their job and invested their money in shares in the company. Their income will now depend on how well the company performs.

Now split them into groups and ask them to come up with professional behaviors that they, as shareholders, would like to see everyone in the company embrace. Ask them to think of behaviors that would contribute to an increase in their share price and the dividends that they receive.

At the end of the group discussions, ask each group to contribute its answers to the whole meeting. Write up a master list of behaviors on a whiteboard. Ask them to agree on the professional behaviors that they wish to become standards. After the meeting, send out a formalized list of the agreed-on professional behaviors to be actively adhered to.

BENEFIT • Helps change staff members' perspectives
• Creates ownership of change through involvement

SOURCE Mark Stanley

The Gold Card

Often, the workplace consists of different teams with different job functions and responsibilities. It is great to be able to involve the teams in a common motivational activity that shows appreciation of and congratulates the professionalism and achievements of all.

PURPOSE
• To recognize the achievements of each team in specific target areas

GROUP SIZE
10 to 50 people

RESOURCE
Gold cards (laminate gold cardboard or ask your local printer to make them), numbered on the back

METHOD
Each team manager sets targets over the month. These targets can involve any area where a behavioral change or productivity measure is sought. The measures may be arbitrary or subjective. They can be individual targets for each team member, a target for each person or a team target. Examples include:
1. opening new accounts
2. receiving a compliment from a customer
3. achieving a certain volume of work
4. learning a new procedure or product
5. meeting a sales target

As each person in the team achieves the target for the period, they are given a gold card. Their name is recorded on a sheet of paper, along with the number of the gold card they received and the reason why they were awarded the gold card. Each fortnight or month, all the teams come together and everyone who has won a gold card puts them in the bowl for the draw. The number of prizes that are drawn depends on the number of people participating. As a person's name is drawn out of the bowl, their accomplishment is read out to the group at large and they are awarded their prize.

PRIZE
Prizes ranging in value between $25 and $50

BENEFIT
• Creates a fun way that anyone can win

SOURCE
Karen Kearney

3 ACHIEVING
GREATER SALES

Imagine your staff increasing sales by 50% in a month, simply by playing a game that costs $50! Or imagine customer service staff suddenly becoming enthusiastic and successful at cross-selling. These are the types of results that managers have achieved through creating simple sales contests and fun games.

The Punters Club

Often, it is just a matter of using a game to help staff to focus on the obvious—more sales. Even though you may have other company bonuses in place, it is always fun to have another game to keep interest stimulated. A leader at a stock brokerage call center devised the 'Punters Club' and got great results.

PURPOSE • To motivate staff to stay on the phone during busy periods in order to take more sales or trades, while at the same time maintaining accuracy

GROUP SIZE 5 to 10 people

RESOURCE Whiteboard or cardboard and pens to keep track of scores

METHOD The objective is to obtain 100 points. Each sale or trade is worth 1 point. Each error is worth minus 10 points. The first person to reach 100 points is declared the winner. Second place and third place prizes are also given for the next 2 people to reach 100 points. If no one reaches 100 points, then the person with the most points at the end of the week is declared the winner.

PRIZE First place: 2 hours off and a bottle of champagne; second place: 1 hour off and a bottle of champagne; third place: a bottle of champagne

BENEFIT • More sales
• More accuracy
• More fun

SOURCE Craig Phillips

Everyone's a Winner

A branch manager was asked to consolidate 3 branches of a leading bank. He was faced with the prospect of bringing together staff from 3 different locations, motivating staff who were disgruntled because of the change, and keeping staff happy as construction in the new branch became a fact of daily life. This task took an innovative solution.

PURPOSE
- To motivate all staff to become sales people
- To increase productivity in 3 target areas
- To bring together people from different departments or branches in a new location

GROUP SIZE   20 to 40 people divided into teams

RESOURCE   Charts or graphs to track progress in the 3 target areas

METHOD   Divide staff into equal teams and give each team the name of a color from the company colors. The teams are then organised by management so that the teams have equal numbers of people from the different locations.

Give each team the targets that it needs to achieve each month in the 3 areas. These targets are converted into a points system. Members of each team accumulate points for the team as well as their own individual points. Allocate points for each sale in each target category. For example, in a target category where sales are of a lower dollar value, allocate 1 point per sale. In a more difficult category, each sale may be worth 3 points. If the team reaches its target of points, then the members of that team can convert their individual points into prizes.

Each team should include people who identify leads and people who convert these leads into sales. For example, in a bank, the tellers identify the leads and the customer service representatives from the same team convert the leads into sales. If a lead is converted into a sale, both the teller and the customer service representative are awarded equal points.

If there are several part-time workers, keep the points system fair by adjusting it so that everyone is on an equal footing. If there is conflict between teams as to who made a sale, then no one receives any points.

In order to further stimulate performance, post the best performance of the top branches or retail outlets. For example, in a bank it could be areas such as deposits, lending and insurance. This can be used as a benchmark for top performance. Each month, the branch or outlet can attempt to beat the top performers in the various areas of performance.

Have a 15-minute meeting each week to review the performance of the previous week. Select staff members to present the results in the 3 different performance areas.

PRIZE   Time off, or prizes within your budget that staff would be motivated to work towards

BENEFIT   • Overall performance in the 3 targeted areas:
1. People who never sold became top sales people
2. Part-timers became the most productive staff members
3. Happy staff working together

SOURCE   Craig Tracey

Cross-Sell Poker

A bank branch manager used the concept of poker to stimulate his branch members to cross-sell products and services to existing customers. The staff had a lot of fun and achieved results that surprised even them.

PURPOSE
- To encourage staff to cross-sell to existing customers
- To increase business through cross-selling

GROUP SIZE 5 to 20 people

RESOURCE 1 or 2 decks of cards, depending on the number of players and the number of cross-sales targeted

METHOD The game is very simple and lots of fun. Each successful cross-sale by a staff member allows them 1 draw from a deck of cards. In order to claim any prize they need to have attained 5 cross-sales in order to draw 5 cards. If they have earned more than 5 chances to draw cards, then they earn the right to discard and draw again until all their allocated cards are used.

At the end of each week everyone meets to draw their cards and collect prizes. Each possible combination is allotted a prize. For example, a pair may earn the staff member a candy bar, three of a kind may entitle them to a movie ticket, or a straight could mean a bottle of champagne.

PRIZE Any small prizes under $10 that staff would enjoy—include one big prize, such as dinner for two, in the event that someone gets four of a kind or has the best hand for the week

BENEFIT
- Keeps up spirits as staff anticipate the cross-sell poker game at the end of the week
- Increases business significantly

SOURCE Bryan Young

Mission Control

A team leader in telephone lending at a direct bank was skimming through *The Fun Factor* one day. While reading about the games that other people had created she was inspired to create this game. Her goal was to get her team to work together to achieve more sales and to encourage them to analyze and plan for the results they hoped to achieve. At the end of the game she asked all her staff to complete a survey on the game.

PURPOSE
- To obtain more sales on the phone
- To build teamwork
- To get people to work smart by analyzing and planning

GROUP SIZE 8 people, working in pairs

RESOURCE Pack containing Mission Announcement (see page 90), Mission Acceptance Form (see page 91), Captain's Proposed Daily Flight Path (see page 92), Lieutenant's Daily Log (see page 93), and Mission Not So Impossible Survey (see page 94)

METHOD The manager pairs up the players in each of the 4 teams, so that the ability level of each team is similar. While the main objective of the game is to obtain the most sales, it is also important that the pairs work as a team and really think about the planning and analysis that is necessary to achieve the required results.

The manager becomes Mission Control. About a week before the game, Mission Control sends out a pack to each team (see pages 90–4). This includes:
1. the Mission Announcement
2. the Mission Acceptance Form
3. the Captain's Proposed Daily Flight Path
4. the Lieutenant's Daily Log
5. the Mission Not So Impossible Survey

At the end of each day, each team submits its Lieutenant's Daily Log to Mission Control and has a 5-minute discussion of its progress. The results of each team are kept secret from the other teams. At the end of each week, the Captains submit their Proposed Daily Flight Path to Mission Control and each team has a meeting with Mission Control to look at strategies for the second week.

At the end of the second week, Mission Control asks each team to complete the Mission Not So Impossible Survey and hand in its final results. Mission Control tabulates the results. As the teams are not aware of each other's progress, the announcement of the winning team is a complete surprise.

PRIZE Keep the prize a secret until the day of the presentation. Give congratulations and feedback to all the players. Present a bottle of wine to each member of the winning team.

BENEFIT • The participants' responses to the survey were very positive. They loved the game and would play it again. The sales they achieved as teams for the 2 weeks were higher than in other teams in the direct banking center during that period.

SOURCE Raz Babic

Dear

You have been paired together to fly your fighter jet home safely. The journey will take you 2 weeks to complete. Along the way your mission will be to obtain the most sales. But be careful, because there are another 3 jets out there aiming for the same results.

What will bring you results is how effectively you work together as a team. To assist you along the way one of you will be the Captain and the other will be the Lieutenant. The role of the Captain will be to organize your flight path each day and the role of the Lieutenant will be to complete the log books.

In your pack you will find blank log sheets that need to be completed each day and given to Mission Control so that contact is never lost. At the start of each day, the Captain will have 10 minutes to brief the Lieutenant on the path for the day using the Captain's Proposed Daily Flight Path. At the end of the day, the Lieutenant will have 10 minutes to record the results and strategies for the day in the Lieutenant's Daily Log and give this to Mission Control.

At the end of the journey, should you be the successful team to have the most sales and have worked the best together, a prize awaits you.

Make it so.

Signing off from Mission Control,

MISSION ACCEPTANCE FORM

Captain _____

Lieutenant _____

Team name _____

Team logo _____

We understand the mission before us and will pursue our goal.

_____   _____

Captain's Proposed Daily Flight Path

Date	Today's action plan	Today's results
Monday		
Tuesday		
Wednesday		
Thursday		
Friday		

Lieutenant's Daily Log

Number of sales opportunities	
Number of sales in progress	
Number of sales completed	

Success story of the day	

Concern for the day	

Sales phrases used	

Suggestions for tomorrow	

Lieutenant _____   Captain _____

Mission Not So Impossible Survey

Team Name: _____

Name:

1. What skill or quality did your team mate(s) display that impressed you? If you had more than one team mate record their name.

2. What skill or quality of your own would you like to pass on to your team mate(s)?

3. What did you learn from this exercise?

4. What would you change about this exercise if you had to do it again?

THANK YOU FOR THE EFFORT YOU PUT INTO COMPETING AND REMEMBER
THAT TO BE THE BEST IS TO DO THE BEST YOU CAN. IN MY EYES YOU HAVE ALL BEEN WINNERS.

The Legend's Productivity Competition

Leon's Legend Team has achieved top productivity month after month in its customer service center. This was accomplished by setting and reaching daily goals for each team member. The weekly 'Productivity Competition' was set in place to maintain the focus and interest of the team members. This technique can be adapted easily to any type of business.

PURPOSE
• To focus daily by setting daily goals for those critical success factors that bring results and can be measured easily

GROUP SIZE
6 to 16 people

RESOURCE
Daily productivity goal and tally sheet to record the staff member's goal in each area and the actual outcomes at the end of the day (see page 97)

METHOD
Explain to your team the value of setting daily goals in the areas that help them to get results. Let them know how important focus and discipline are to increase productivity.

Introduce your plan to incorporate a daily productivity goal and tally sheet for the team to help the team members to increase their productivity. Tell the team that a 5-minute meeting will take place each morning between you and each team member to record their goals for the day in each area and to give them feedback on the previous day's results. It can be valuable to involve the team in the development of the tally sheet, so that staff do not feel that this is being thrust on them.

Discuss what daily goals should be set for each team member and how these goals can be accomplished. In a call center, the software package should provide the statistics to record the daily productivity of each team member. In an office situation, each person may need to record their own accomplishments each day.

Leon's Legend Team identified 4 critical success areas:
1. calls per hour
2. accuracy

3. cross-sales

4. sales conversions

To implement the daily goals into the team's daily routine, introduce a competition called the 'Legend's Productivity Competition'. Divide the participants into smaller teams of 4 people for a 1-week competition. Score the teams on a points basis. In each of the 4 critical success areas, award points as follows: 1: 10 points; 2: 7 points; 3: 5 points; and 4: 2 points.

If a team member is away on sick leave for 1 or 2 days without a doctor's note, the team loses 10 point per day. If a team member is away on sick leave for 1 or 2 days with a doctor's note, the team loses 5 points. If a team member has no sick leave in the week, 20 bonus points are given to the team. If a team member is on long-term sick leave (anything over 3 days), the team does not lose points but it does not gain bonus points.

At the end of each week, the team with the most points is announced as the winner. A monthly prize is given to the best overall individual performance, based on the most points earned.

REWARD A perpetual trophy for the weekly competition; the monthly winner is given the 'Oscar Award' for the best performance in a customer service center (see page 98), as well as 2 movie tickets.

BENEFIT • Gives clarity to team members about what it is important to focus on
• Helps promote team morale and lifts the spirit of fun
• The whole team more easily maintains top performance status

SOURCE Leon Thompson

Goal and Tally Sheet

Date: _____ Team: _____

Name: _____

	Goal	Result	Goal	Result	Goal	Result	Goal	Result
Monday								
Tuesday								
Wednesday								
Thursday								
Friday								

Congratulations

_____

You have won the

OSCAR AWARD

for the
Best Overall Individual
Performance
for the month of

_____

Signed _____

5-Card Draw

Whenever you need a quick game to boost productivity that costs nothing and only requires a pack of cards, the game '5-Card Draw' is the answer. A quick-thinking and clever team leader helped his team have *fun* and *gains* with this simple strategy.

PURPOSE
• To increase sales conversions with every customer enquiry

GROUP SIZE
4 to 8 people, or 9 to 16 people

RESOURCE
1 pack of playing cards for 4 to 8 people; 2 packs of cards for 9 to 16 people

METHOD
On a central table, display the deck of playing cards in suits and in order face up. Explain to your staff that each time they convert an enquiry into a sale they can choose any card that is still available in the deck. Their objective is to get the best 5-card draw poker hand over the period of time in which the game is played. In order to achieve this they will also be aware of what type of hands other staff members are trying to create because the cards are already taken. The fun is to get the best hand possible, but also to pick those cards that will stop others from getting a better hand than theirs. At the end of the game the person with the best 5-card draw poker hand wins.

REWARD
The fun of winning the game

BENEFIT
• Helps focus the attention on sales
• Creates fun and immediate results

SOURCE
Matthew Oswald

The Team Challenge

One team in a customer service center decided to challenge another team in order to lift its production. The team members picked a team that was at a similar performance level to their own. This same game could be used in a retail outlet or a branch of a large organization. Simply challenge another branch or retail store that is similar in performance.

PURPOSE
- To work together as a team to lift productivity levels by challenging another team or branch that is similar in performance

GROUP SIZE Team, branch or retail store of any size

RESOURCE Scoreboard and team banner

METHOD
1. Select a day each week for 3 weeks that you will compete on. It may be the slowest or busiest day, or even a special campaign day.
2. Determine the areas of performance that will be measured and assign points to each area. For example, in a customer service phone center the team may be given:
5 points for each person who takes 100 calls
10 points for each person who takes 150 calls
1 point for each 5 sales
Put up a team banner and mark the points on the scoreboard. The team with the most points on the day wins. The team with the best score over the best out of 3 days is the final winner.

PRIZE The losing team provides the winning team's prize.

BENEFIT
- Helps develop teamwork, team pride and lifts everyone's spirits
- Stimulates people to attain new levels of productivity as they strive to beat their own score from the previous game

SOURCE Narelle Nelson

The Tennis Tournament

A fun and easy way to motivate sales and service staff is to hold a sales contest that takes place the same time as a well-known tennis tournament such as Wimbledon, the French Open, the Australian Open or the U.S. Open. The sales contest is run along the same lines as a tennis tournament.

PURPOSE • To increase sales during the time that a major tennis tournament is being held

GROUP SIZE 8 to 16 people

RESOURCE Whiteboard or bulletin board and cut-outs of tennis rackets (see page 103)

METHOD Determine what area of performance to use as a measure. You may choose the most sales, the most dollar value, the highest customer satisfaction rating or the most cross-sales. The person who scores highest in the designated performance area each day will win the set. The best of 3 or 5 days (each day represents a set) wins the match. The winner moves on to play in the next round. To keep everyone aware of who is playing who and their progress, use cut-outs of tennis rackets with team names added as markers to track performance.

1. Divide staff into 2 groups. Each player competes with the others in their group over 15 to 20 days. The winner of each of the groups plays in the finals.

2. All players play in the first round. Each round lasts for 3 to 5 days. Match the players against each other by drawing from a hat.

3. In the second round, the winners of the first round draw again for their opponents.

4. During the semi-finals, divide the staff members who are out of the game into supporters for each of the final 2 players of their group. As supporters they will provide encouragement, banners and cheerleading for their player.

5. The grand final is held on the final 3 to 5 days of the competition. If possible, ensure the final day of the competition corresponds with the final day of the tennis

tournament that you are following. Each group will now get behind its player, encouraging and supporting them to final victory.

For additional interest and fun, have each player draw the name of the top tennis players at the international tournament that you are following. The person who draws the winner of the tournament also wins a prize.

PRIZE Reward the winner with a gift voucher and trophy, and give a prize for second place. Provide a small prize for each member of the winner's group and for the person who drew the name of the winner of the international tournament.

BENEFIT
- Helps everyone improve their sales results and sales techniques
- People share their techniques with others and offer encouragement to their team members

SOURCE Manfred Granig

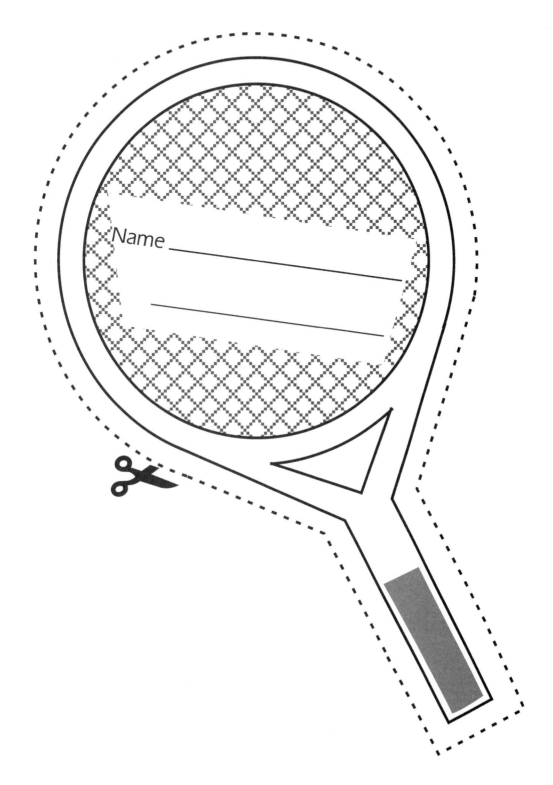

Name

5-Star Sales and Service

Doing business by phone today often requires sales or customer service representatives to call prospective customers or existing customers to offer information, set up appointments and introduce new products or services. Often, when these calls are made the person making the call is not clear on their objectives. When they understand their objectives and can obtain even part of their objectives, they start to feel successful and are encouraged to persist and improve. The following activity is used to help people to have a clear understanding of their objectives and to feel successful for each and every call.

PURPOSE
- To encourage and help sales and service people in the quantity and quality of their calls to customers

GROUP SIZE
Any number

RESOURCE
Individual scoresheets and a scoreboard for players

METHOD
Identify with your team members 5 to 6 objectives that you would like each person to achieve for each call that is made to an existing customer or to a prospective customer. Such objectives might include making contact with the client, leaving a message, making an appointment to call back, making a presentation, gaining information, sending a proposal, quote or information, or receiving a payment. Assign stars to these objectives in order of their importance to rate the call success. For example:

CALL SUCCESS
★ ★ ★ ★ ★

Made contact	1 star
Left a message	1 star
Arranged to call back	1 star
Made a presentation	2 stars
Sent a proposal	$1\frac{1}{2}$ stars
Received a payment	2 stars

The ultimate goal is to make as many $4^{1}/_{2}$- or 5-star calls as possible each day. A competition can be created based on the most 5-star calls per person or per team, or it can be created by counting the number of stars that team members achieve for each of the objective areas per hour. For example:

Contact rate: number of contacts per hour

Effective call rate: number of sales presentations per hour

Effective sales rate: number of commitments per hour

Give everyone an individual score sheet and track their progress daily on the whiteboard.

PRIZE   Provide a prize based on something to do with stars or with stars on it, for example movie tickets to see the winner's favorite movie star. For a longer competition, offer dinner or accommodation in a 5-star hotel.

BENEFIT   • People feel successful with almost every call that they make because they achieve stars for the call. This will act as a form of reward and recognition.

SOURCE   Carolyn Greenwich

Roulette Royale

The team leader who created Roulette Royale was reward by royal-sized results. In the first month he had a 97% increase in business. It only cost him $50!

PURPOSE
- To increase cross-sales and general sales results in an outbound telesales team (the game can be adapted to meet any productivity goal)

GROUP SIZE 6 to 20 people

RESOURCE A roulette wheel, roulette chips and a pack of cards; any visual decorations to record the progress of each player that would appeal to the staff in the office

METHOD Determine the number of sales and cross-sales that the sales or customer service consultants need to accumulate to win a roulette chip. If you have both full-time and part-time staff, make the number for part-time staff about two-thirds that for full-time staff. For example, if full-time staff need to get 15 sales or cross-sales to win a roulette chip, part-time staff will need 10 sales or cross-sales. Record the results for all to see.

Each time a staff member accumulates enough sales for a chip, they earn the right to spin the roulette wheel for a prize. Each number on the wheel corresponds to a different prize. If the number has been spun before, they spin again until they win a prize.

At the end of the month hold a 'Final Play' event. Ask everyone to bring the chips that they have earned and place them on the roulette table to establish the final winner. Staff put their chips on as many different numbers as they like. If there is more than one winner after the first spin, the wheel is spun again until there is only one winner. The final prize is a prize of slightly greater value.

Each week, the team leader awards the random jackpot winner. This person is deemed to have had the most outstanding achievement of the week, the best idea of the week, the biggest or best cross-sale of the week, etc. The winner of this award wins the opportunity to bet for a prize. They can either bet on red or black on the roulette table or they can choose a game of Black Jack against the team leader. If they win, they earn a spin on the roulette wheel and a chip for the Final Play.

PRIZE   36 small-value prizes are needed for each month the game is played (take a trip to a $1 or $2 shop for a range of prizes, and supplement these with $1 or $2 scratchies, candy, movie passes and time-off vouchers).

BENEFIT
- Helps energize the office
- Keeps staff focused on cross-selling
- Helps people realize what they are capable of achieving

SOURCE   Tony Tzoumacas

Balloon Bonanza

This is a quick and easy game that everyone enjoys. It is a game that you can use to help stimulate top results in a special campaign. This game was used to help sell tickets to an Elton John concert.

PURPOSE • To increase the sales of a particular product or service during a campaign

GROUP SIZE 8 to 30 people

RESOURCE Lots of balloons and raffle tickets

METHOD During a special sales campaign decide the dollar value, number of sales, or combination of sales that will win each staff member the right to burst a balloon and win a prize.

On the stub of each raffle ticket, write the prize that will go with that ticket. Put a raffle ticket in each balloon, blow up the balloons and hang them from the ceiling or on the walls of the office for the greatest visual impact.

Each time a staff member earns the right to a prize, they burst a balloon. This can happen any time throughout the day.

PRIZE A range of small-value prizes. Include a few joke prizes and a few high-value prizes. Let the staff know beforehand the general type and value of the prizes, so that their expectations are not dashed.

BENEFIT • Causes excitement and a sense of fun in the office
• Helps bring out a constructive and friendly competitive spirit

SOURCE Judy Purdon

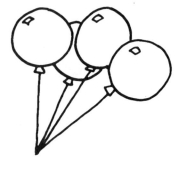

Shipwrecked With the Stars

This is a perfect game to play if you have absolutely no money to spend on visuals or prizes. Everyone in the team at one call center who played this game had lots of fun and got great results as well.

PURPOSE • To help staff to be aware of and develop work habits that produce excellent results

GROUP SIZE Ideal for a team of 6 to 14 people

RESOURCE Whiteboard and markers, magazines

METHOD Each morning, ask each team member to write down their name and the name of a celebrity that they would most like to be shipwrecked with on a tropical island. Ask them not to share the name of their celebrity with any other team members— only you should know the celebrity chosen by each person.

On the whiteboard, draw up a number of columns and write the name of each celebrity in the right-hand column. In each column after that write the area of production that you will be recording. For example, you may wish to record some of the following productivity measures: inbound calls taken, sales conversions, cross-sales, outbound calls made, contacts made, errors made, etc.

Every 2 hours or twice a day, collect the statistics from each person or the system and put them onto the whiteboard in the name of the celebrity instead of the real person. Place a gold star or some other type of indicator against the top performer for the 2-hourly or half-day period. At the end of the day, the person with the best overall statistics is the winner.

You may wish to change the areas or combination of areas that you are competing against on a daily basis, so that more people have a chance of winning.

PRIZE Announce each day's winner the next morning. Cut out a magazine picture of the person, paste it onto a piece of cardboard and present it to the winner.

BENEFIT • Everyone sees the performance of the whole group but they have no idea whose figures they are seeing. The lowest achiever is not put in a position of embarrassment.
• Creates awareness of what is expected and what everyone is achieving

SOURCE Anna Marsh-Quigley

Pot of Gold

An international car rental company was setting up a business center to build up relationships with its existing corporate clients and to win new corporate clients. The group was very comfortable with its regular calls, but a bit reluctant to call new prospects. The manager needed to start developing good work habits that would insure the staff would be productive and came up with this activity.

PURPOSE
- To improve the number of outbound calls to prospective clients, thereby increasing the amount of new business

GROUP SIZE   6 to 10 people

RESOURCE   A large board or piece of butcher's paper for the rainbow, colored felt pens for each player and a picture of a pot of gold for the end of the rainbow

METHOD   Assign each member in the team an individual daily target for new prospect calls and call outcomes according to realistic expectations. Explain that the team target is the total of the individual targets. The regular calls to existing clients still need to be made, but are not part of the game.

Create a points system for the outcome of each call. For example:

Making contact	1 point
Sending out an application	5 points
Opening a new account	10 points

You may set people different targets, so that, for instance, some have a daily target of 25 points and others have a daily target of 40 points.

Ask everyone to choose a color of the rainbow. Draw a large rainbow on the board or butcher's paper and divide the rays into 10 sections, representing the daily goals of each person over the 2-week period. Their objective each day is to reach their target and get their ray of the rainbow closer to the pot of gold. At the end of the day, each person colors in the section of their ray of the rainbow representing the completion of their daily goal. If they have not reached their goal, or they

111

have exceeded their goal, then they color in the approximate area that represents their accomplishment for the day.

The individual winner is the person who reaches the pot of gold first. The team wins the group prize if the team target is reached within the 2-week period. If someone reaches the pot of gold before the end of the 2-week period, they can continue to earn points and give them away to other team members to help the team win as a whole.

PRIZE   Individual prize: CD voucher and certificate (see page 113); team prize: dinner out for everyone

BENEFIT
- Helps build confidence to make outbound calls
- Gives people a fair chance to compete against others while still competing as a team

SOURCE   Louise Fritschy

Thank you

for your
participation
in helping your
department
to achieve its
target

2 months

Go-Cart Gala

A motor insurance company really grabbed the interest of its teams with this simple game that lasted 2 months and got great results.

PURPOSE • To boost sales production and encourage staff to sell new products

GROUP SIZE 20 to 60 people

RESOURCE A tracking board for the race; prizes

METHOD Divide the office into 2 or 3 teams with 10 to 20 people in each team. Organize the teams evenly based on previous sales results, so that all teams are given a fair chance to win. Ask each team to choose a model of a car to represent them. Provide each team with $10 to purchase a small model of the car, or use the cut-outs provided (see page 115).

Organize the race in a points system. For each normal sale made by a team member, the team gets 1 point. For each sale of a new product that you are encouraging the team members to sell, the team gets 2 points.

Design a racetrack on the wall, using Blu-Tack to stick on the racing cars. At the end of each day, move each car according to the number of points that each team has accumulated. The team with the most points at the end of 2 months is the winner.

PRIZE The winning team is awarded a gala day of go-carting and lunch. The overall best performance by a team member is awarded a weekend away for 2 that includes a day of car racing.

SOURCE Janeene Hutchinson

$10 Wish

A call center tried everything to improve sales in a particular product each month. When it tried this quick and easy technique, it got the results it was looking for.

PURPOSE
• To encourage each sales or customer service person to improve their sales in a particular product each month

GROUP SIZE 20 to 100 people

RESOURCE Display of the previous month's sales results; prize

METHOD Determine a particular product that provides a healthy profit margin for the company. It needs to be one that the staff can improve their sales performance in each month.

Announce to staff that each month, if they better their previous month's sales of the chosen product, they will be given a $10 gift certificate. If it seems more appropriate, ask for a specific dollar amount improvement in sales, such as an increase of $100. It is important that staff are only asked to improve on the previous month's sale performance. This way, if their sales drop for a month, they will still be encouraged to strive to improve their sales the next month.

PRIZE $10 gift certificate

BENEFIT
• Staff feel encouraged to sell each month. If they have a bad month, they feel capable of improving the next month; if they have a good month, they feel they can keep on achieving.
• Keeps staff focused on the important products to sell

SOURCE Cherie Stelzer

Christmas Tree Spree

When you need to keep the momentum up during Christmas time, this simple and visual game will be appreciated and enjoyed by all staff.

PURPOSE
• To let people enjoy a visual display of everyone's success and to encourage sales by immediate rewards

GROUP SIZE
8 to 50 people

RESOURCE
Christmas tree, gold Christmas decorations and name tags (see page 118), or a large cut-out tree attached to the wall and gold cut-out decorations, a large box and gifts

METHOD
Display your Christmas tree in an area that everyone can see easily. Next to the tree, place a large box containing the gold decorations, with a name tag attached to each one. If you are using a cut-out tree and cut-out decorations, write the name of each person on the cut-out decorations.

Each time a staff member makes a sale or a number or sales worth a designated dollar amount, they place a decoration on the tree and write their name on the decoration. As the tree becomes more and more decorated, the staff can see the overall sales performance.

Take a trip to the local $1 and $2 shops to purchase lots of inexpensive Christmas tree presents. Depending on the budget, you may wish to include some higher value presents too. Wrap all the presents and place them under the tree. Each time a staff member makes 3 to 5 sales, or achieves a specified dollar amount of sales, they get to choose a present.

REWARD
The fun of decorating the tree and unwrapping presents

BENEFIT
• A fun way to celebrate the Christmas season and encourage sales production at the same time

SOURCE
Cherie Stelzer

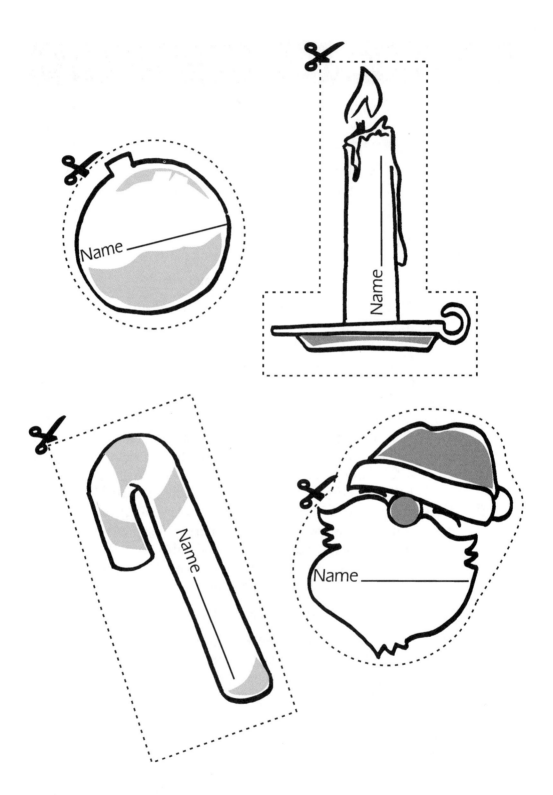

Name _____

Name _____

Name _____

Name _____

A Month at the Races

This game worked wonders for a hotel club marketing group, which wanted to encourage hotel staff to provide referrals for the telephone sales team.

PURPOSE
- To increase sales by referrals and to encourage staff in a position to get referrals to give these to sales staff

GROUP SIZE 5 to 25 people

RESOURCE Whiteboard and pens

METHOD Pair up a telephone sales person with a person who meets customers face to face. For example, match a telephone sales team member with a hotel staff member who meets and talks to customers on a regular basis.

To launch the competition, have a 'get together' for everyone to meet each other and select or be assigned their partner for the competition.

The objective of the game is to see which pair of players can achieve the most sales through referrals. Every time a face-to-face customer service person provides a lead to a telephone sales person that is converted into a sale, the pair get 1 point. Create a visual tracking system on the whiteboard showing daily race results.

The pair with the most points at the end of the month wins.

PRIZE Dinner for two for each member of the winning pair

BENEFIT
- Both the telephone sales person and the face-to-face customer service person develop a greater appreciation and understanding of the other's responsibilities and achievements
- A valuable opportunity to get referrals is not lost

SOURCE Janelle Wallace

Baskets of Referrals

Most sales managers know that one of the best times to get referrals for potential new sales is when a sale has just been made. A hotel club marketing group developed a fun and unique way to capitalize on these opportunities.

PURPOSE • To increase sales and increase referral leads

GROUP SIZE 2 teams of between 10 to 20 people each

RESOURCE Scoreboard and pens

METHOD Divide the office into 2 teams. If there is a morning shift and an afternoon shift, put half of each shift into each team. Ask the teams to pick the name of a local or national basketball team as their team name. If the budget allows, buy 2 basketball shirts emblazoned with the team names to display next to the scoreboard.

Each sale made by the team equals 1 point for the team. Each referral lead from each sale also equals 1 point. You will need to check these referrals to insure their validity. This can be done easily by announcing that spot checks will be made on a number of referral leads.

Choose a team captain for each team—someone who is not a top performer. This person's job is to encourage the team, track their performance and write the total points for the day or shift each day on the scoreboard.

At the end of the 1- or 2-week period, the team with the most points wins. The teams vote for the best and fairest player on each team, and you award the 'man of the match'.

PRIZE The team prize is lunch or breakfast for the team. The best and fairest player receives a certificate (see page 121) and 2 movie tickets, and the player of the match receives a prize of their choice, worth $50.

BENEFIT • Helps people to develop the habit of asking for referrals

SOURCE Janelle Wallace

_____

is voted as the
Best and Fairest
Player
by their peers

Signed by their peers

_____

_____

_____

_____

_____

Clueless

This game was enjoyed by all the telephone sales staff at a credit union. It was so much fun that the staff decided they would like to have a game every week to look forward to. The manager was happy about this, but told them that they would have to take turns inventing a different game!

PURPOSE • To stimulate sales through a fun guessing game

GROUP SIZE 10 to 18 people

RESOURCE The 26 letters of the alphabet on 10 cm^2 cut-outs, whiteboard or corkboard, candy bars and fruit

METHOD Select a 5-letter word that 5 people will win the opportunity to try to guess at the end of the day. You may also wish to provide a clue. For example, if the word is 'water', your clue could be HIJKLMNO—the keys to this clue are the first and last letters of the clue standing for H_2O.

It is also fun not to include a clue and to pick a 5-letter word that can be used to spell a number of words.

At the top of the whiteboard, write the title of the game: 'Clueless'. If you are to provide a clue, write this under the title. Working down the whiteboard, draw 5 blank circles, which are to be filled in at the end of the day. At the bottom of the whiteboard, write the 26 letters of the alphabet.

Next to the whiteboard place a bowl with the cut-out letters, a bowl filled with a selection of candy bars and a bowl of fruit.

Announce to the staff that each time they make a sale they are able to choose a letter and reward themselves with a candy bar or a piece of fruit until all the letters are taken. At the end of the day, you will announce the 5 winning letters. The 5 people who hold a winning letter will have an opportunity to guess the word. Hold a draw to determine the order of guessing. If a person has one or more of the winning letters, they will get more than one chance to guess. The person who guesses the word first wins the game.

PRIZE Anything under the value of $10, such as a movie ticket or a bottle of wine. If you decide to have a different game each week, you may like to make or purchase a trophy to sit on the desk of the winner until the next daily game.

BENEFIT • Adds interests and enthusiasm to the day
• Boosts sales for the day as everyone competes for a letter

SOURCE Jann Fenley

$50 Fiesta

By the end of the month, this telephone sales center had its walls and windows plastered with $50 play notes. Sales had taken a big boost for the month as well.

PURPOSE • To increase sales over a month

GROUP SIZE 5 to 20 people

RESOURCE A stack of play $50 notes (see page 125), photocopied in a variety of colors

METHOD Give each member of the team or office the same number of $50 notes. If you have more than 10 people, have the staff work in pairs, and select the pairs so that everyone has an equal chance to win. Each team member or pair should be given a particular color of notes.

Tell the staff that each time they make a sale, they get to Blu-Tack or tape one $50 note anywhere on the wall. As the month progresses, the walls and windows will become covered in $50 notes of various colors. Some of the staff may even start to make designs or figures out of the notes.

At the end of the month, the person or pair with the most notes on the wall is declared the winner.

Ask the staff how they would like to dispose of the $50 notes at the end of the month. The staff of the sales office that created the game chose to gather all the notes together, toss them in the air and then wad and stamp through the fake money as it fell to the floor.

PRIZE $50 for the winner or winning pair

BENEFIT • Provides a great visual impact of success
• Using a different color of notes for each person or pair gives staff an opportunity to see their progress compared to others in the team

SOURCE Jann Fenley

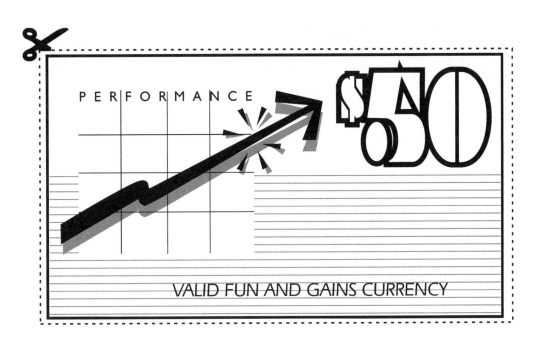

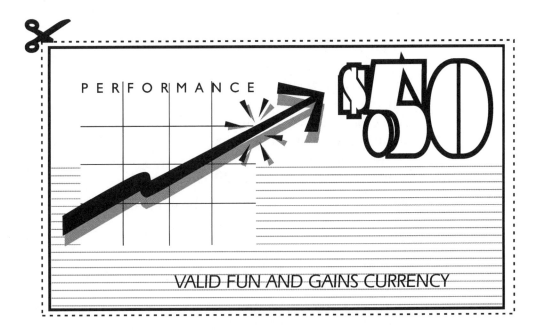

Bingo

This is a fun and easy game to play any day of the week. The fund management company that used this game found that, in order to achieve success with the game, it needed to make it relatively easy to reach bingo.

PURPOSE
• To improve sales in 5 different areas

GROUP SIZE
5 to 25 people

RESOURCE
Bingo cards with space to fill in the 5 letters of the word 'bingo'

METHOD
Select 5 different types and quantities of sales or sales behavior that you would like your staff to accomplish in the course of a day. Assign each one of these sales or sales behaviors a letter in the word BINGO. For example:

B   1 sale over $500
I   5 sales of a particular item
N   10 outbound calls made to clients
G   10 sales (the 5 sales of a particular item can be included in the total of 10)
O   2 referrals

Give every staff member a bingo card (see page 127). Every time someone accomplishes one of these sales or behaviors, they put a cross through the appropriate letter on their bingo card. Once a person accomplishes all 5, they yell out 'Bingo!'. The first person to yell out 'Bingo!' for the day wins. Everyone else who subsequently achieves bingo also yells it out and they go into a draw for a prize at the end of the day.

PRIZE
Movie tickets for the first place winner and the winner of the draw

BENEFIT
• Helps staff to focus on the most important results for the day
• Creates good work habits as staff organize their day to achieve results
• Creates a competitive spirit, but also allows everyone who spells 'bingo' to have the chance to win a prize

SOURCE
Tracey Flynn

LETTER	ACHIEVEMENT	DATE/ TIME
B		
I		
N		
G		
O		

Team Target Tangle

To motivate teams by means of a healthy competition, the manager of a home loan company devised this interesting and comprehensive competition that lasted 3 months.

PURPOSE • To increase productivity in 5 target areas

GROUP SIZE 2 to 10 teams of 4 to 10 people

RESOURCE Chocolate wheel to spin for bonus points or prizes, and whiteboard to post results

METHOD Divide the office into 2 to 10 equal teams of 4 to 10 people. Set up 5 target areas in which you wish to increase productivity and assign points to each area. For example:

1. *Customer management target* A new lead must be called within 3 hours of receiving the lead or 3 attempts must be made within 24 hours to contact the lead. Failure to meet this customer management target for each lead results in minus 25 points.

2. *Percentage of weekly or monthly sales target reached* Assign points that coincide with the percentage of the target met. For example, 85% of the target met equals 85 points, 110% equals 110 points, etc. No points are received if less than 80% of the target is met.

3. *Approved sales* Each approved sale earns the person a spin of the chocolate wheel for points. Place a range of points on the wheel, including a number of instances of 20, 40 and 50, one of 100 and one of minus 10. You may wish to include a few prizes on the board too, instead of points.

4. *Lead conversions* Evenly distribute the leads between staff. For each lead that is converted into a sale, give 25 points, plus a spin on the chocolate wheel.

5. *Time management* Many companies are able to monitor the amount of time logged on the phone. If the person meets this weekly criteria, give 25 points.

On the whiteboard, log the individual team's points as they progress on a day-to-day basis and post the teams' results weekly.

At the end of 3 months, the team with the most points wins. The person with the best overall score also wins a prize.

PRIZE The team prize is an activity that the team members can all do together and that everyone enjoys, such as a golf day, a picnic or a day cruise. Choose something that is within budget but reflects what the team has accomplished without being so extravagant that it causes jealously from other teams. For the individual winner provide a weekend away for two.

BENEFIT • Team competitions are a wonderful utilization of peer pressure and peer support
• Keeps everyone informed of the progress of the whole office
• Stimulates good work habits

SOURCE Paul Kennedy

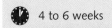

3-D Puzzle

This very visual game was a huge success and lots of fun for the teams that competed against each other at the call center of a major bank. This game can be used in almost any office, branch or retail outlet. All you need to purchase are a number of 3-D puzzles, which can be found at toy stores.

PURPOSE
- To encourage customer service staff to identify and act on cross-selling opportunities with existing customers
- To boost sales through a team competition for telephone sales representatives or retail sales people

GROUP SIZE 3 to 4 teams of 3 to 10 players

RESOURCE A 3-D puzzle for each team and a large table to display the puzzles; prizes

METHOD Divide the office into 3 to 4 equal teams of 3 to 10 people. The objective of this game is to see which team can build its puzzle first. Have each team select the puzzle of its choice. Place a table in an area that is easily seen from most areas in the office. If the game is being played in a retail store, place a table in the staffroom. Set out the boxes with the puzzles and assign an area on the table for each team to construct its puzzle. Ask the teams to adopt a team name for the competition. The teams may also wish to decorate their team area with the theme of their puzzle. To start with, give out only 5 pieces of each puzzle, the picture of the completed puzzle and the instructions. (In the event that there are a different number of pieces in each puzzle, make the adjustment by giving out those extra pieces in the first week, so that all teams start on an equal footing.)

Next, determine how many pieces of puzzle each sale or cross-sale is worth. For example, you may decide that each sale is worth 5 pieces of puzzle, or that each $100 worth of sales is worth 5 pieces. Award the team with the most sales each day a bonus of 5 to 10 pieces of puzzle. The person who has the most sales for the day also wins an additional 5 pieces of puzzle for their team. At the end of each week, tally up the number of pieces of puzzle that each team has won.

After work or on the break the next morning, let the teams assemble the puzzle with the pieces they have won.

The game is over when the first team completes its puzzle. Keep the game going until all puzzles are complete.

PRIZE   Award $100 to be spent as the team wishes, and award $50 to the best overall individual performer.

BENEFIT
- Gives a visual display of success as the puzzles are assembled
- Creates a fun, non-threatening team competition
- Builds team spirit

SOURCE   Stacey Watson

Jelly Bean Jar

When the administration department is under pressure to meet a heavy volume of work and the deadline is looming ahead, a game to lighten the mood may be the best way to lift everyone's spirits.

PURPOSE • To provide staff with a visual display of the work completed and the targets yet to be accomplished

GROUP SIZE Ideally 10 to 20 people, but this activity can be adapted easily to a larger sized group

RESOURCE Very large, tall glass jar or container

METHOD Find a very large and very tall glass jar or container. Mark off the days with a felt marker for a 2-week deadline or the weeks for a 4- to 8-week deadline. Divide up the amount of work that is to be accomplished in that time frame and then write these amounts next to the days or weeks that have been marked on the jar, such as 100, 200, 300, etc.

Depending on the amount of work or the type of work to be achieved, it may be better to divide the department into teams. Make sure everyone knows what the team target is and the individual part each person will need to contribute. Each team has its own jelly bean jar to fill.

At the end of the day or week, fill up the jar with jelly beans or candy to show the amount of work that has been accomplished. To make the jar more visually interesting, you could choose a different type of candy for each target period.

The team that reaches its target first can receive an additional team prize.

PRIZE Provide everyone with a bag of candy from the jelly bean jar. Alternatively, buy or make a piñata (a Mexican animal made of papier-mâché). Pour all the wrapped candies and some extra mini chocolate bars into the piñata. When the deadline has been met, get everyone together for a deadline party with refreshments. Blindfold all the staff in turn, giving each person the opportunity to hit and break the piñata with a light weight or toy baseball bat.

BENEFIT
- A fun way for teams to reach targets
- Creates team spirit and teamwork

SOURCE Brenda Shields

The Big Day Out

Sometimes, when staff have a productivity goal that stretches over a few months, they can lose momentum unless there are smaller goals to reach along the way. This is the clever way one teleservices company kept its staff enthusiasm and productivity humming away.

PURPOSE
- To reach a longer-term target by setting and rewarding smaller goals along the way

GROUP SIZE
8 to 80 people (for more than 8 people, divide the participants into teams)

RESOURCE
Pictures of picnic food

METHOD
Communicate the target that the department needs to reach to meet the budget or deadline, then divide that target into weekly targets over the 6 to 12-week period.

Invite everyone to a 'Big Day Out' at a park or beach at the end of the game period. This will give everyone plenty of advance notice. Tell everyone that, to make the big day out really special, it would probably be a good idea to have food, and explain that each week they will have the opportunity to win different food items for the big day out by meeting their monthly targets.

Ask the group what food they would enjoy for the picnic and then divide the menu into the weeks of the game. For example:

Week 1	BBQ chickens, ham, etc.
Week 2	Cases of soft drink
Week 3	Salads, rolls and bread
Week 4	Cases of beer
Week 5	Wine and champagne
Week 6	Chips and dips
Week 7	Ice-cream
Week 8	Cakes and deserts

Each week that the goal is met, put up visual displays of the food that has been won for the big day out. If you have divided the group into teams, provide something extra for the team that has performed the best.

On the big day out, have staff organize games and races such as the ever-popular beanbag race or sack-race. Provide small prizes for each winner.

PRIZE The big day out is the reward for all. For weekly team prizes shop at a toy or sports store for outdoor games such as horse shoes, a baseball and bat, and beanbags that can be used for games or for fun at the big day out.

BENEFIT
- Unbelievable team motivation and morale
- The team works hard together to make sure the targets are met
- A great day to anticipate and to remember

SOURCE Brenda Shields

Race Around the World

One bank's call center was keen to get customers who phoned in to register to use the phone banking service. The managers got together and devised this 3-month game, which brought in greater results than they could have hoped for.

PURPOSE
• To get customer service representatives to focus on achieving a specific result over and above their usual tasks

GROUP SIZE
6 teams of 10 to 20 people

RESOURCE
A world map, team tags (see page 138) and marker

METHOD
Each team competes against the other teams in a race around the world, and each team member competes to reach their individual target. Start by assigning each team a different route around the world with 12 weekly destination spots. The teams' objective each week is to reach their target so that they can move on to the next destination on their predetermined itinerary. To reach this objective, the teams need to meet their targets, which could be, for example:
1. registering existing customers to use a new service
2. cross-selling a specific product
3. obtaining a referral
4. selling a specific dollar amount

Place the world map on a wall and plot the progress of each team. Each Friday morning, post the statistics for the previous week onto the wall next to the map.

Every team that has reached its target is asked to bring in a souvenir from the place it has reached. A photograph is taken of the team members with their souvenir and this is posted on the wall. The team is then given its new destination with a target to aim for the next week.

Each week, the member of each team with the best results is awarded a cash prize. In order to make it fair for part-time employees, score this on a percentage basis so that everyone is equal.

PRIZE $25 cash for the top producing team member in each team each week. At the end of the 3 months, award $300 to the winning team to spend as the team wishes. Award the best overall individual performer a weekend away for two.

BENEFIT   • Promotes teamwork and encourages non-competitive people to get results for the benefit of the team
• Stimulates competitive people who are motivated by winning the weekly prize

SOURCE   Barbara Kernos

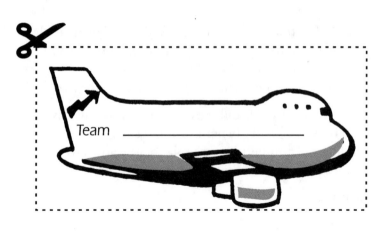

Team _____

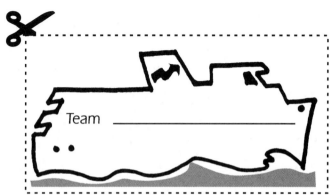

Team _____

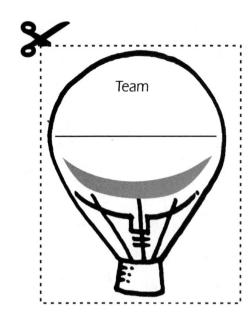

Team _____

Team

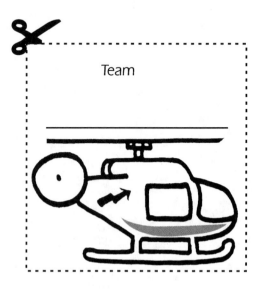

Surprise Competitions

Having competitions all the time can become tedious. Knowing when the competition is going to happen can take away the spontaneity. One direct marketing company decided to always keep sales staff guessing. No one knew whether or not there would be a competition on that day until they arrived for work.

PURPOSE
- To give a boost to sales results over and above what is encouraged through the normal and ongoing incentives or commissions

GROUP SIZE 10 to 30 people

RESOURCE Whiteboard and pens

METHOD Twice a week, hold a competition for 4 hours. Do not announce what the competition is and the prizes that can be won until just before the competition is played. Here are two competitions that get great results.

Mystery Numbers

On a whiteboard, write up the target number of sales for the competition. For example, if the target is 50 sales, the number 50 would be written in big letters on the whiteboard. Underneath the target number, write each number between 1 and that number. Five of these numbers are then chosen as the mystery numbers. Each time a person makes a sale, they call out the next number on the whiteboard and a line is put through that number to indicate the number of sales achieved. If that number is one of the 5 mystery numbers, that person wins one of the daily prizes.

The Best Team Wins

When people arrive at work, give them a number between 1 and 4. This number will designate the team that they are on for the competition. On the whiteboard, write up each team's target sales number for the competition. At the end of the competition, the team that has come closest to the target or that has exceeded the target the most, wins a prize for each team member.

PRIZE   Any prize under the value of $10 such as wine, pens, chocolates, movie tickets or gift vouchers.

BENEFIT   • Energizes the staff instantaneously
          • Creates fun and competition while giving everyone a chance to win

SOURCE   Trevor Harvey and Kym Eveleigh

Operation Countdown

Not everyone enjoys competitions. To devise a competition that everyone can win and become motivated by is what one entertainment marketing company wanted to do to sell tickets for a major musical event. The game involved the whole department, and kept people on target and motivated as they worked towards selling thousands of tickets.

PURPOSE • To help everyone, whether they enjoy competitions or not, to reach a specific sales target as a team

GROUP SIZE 5 to 100 people

RESOURCE 2 large bowls and tickets with prizes written on them; prizes

METHOD Determine the number of units you wish your customer service or sales team to sell. For each 10 units to be sold, put a ticket with a prize written on it in a large bowl for everyone to see. For example, if you had 10 000 units as the target for the campaign, the bowl would contain 1000 tickets with prizes written on them. Each time a person sells 10 units they are able to draw a ticket and collect their prize. The person then writes their name on the ticket and places the ticket into another bowl for the draw for the major prize at the end of the campaign.

The bowls of tickets, both those that have been won and those still to be won, let everyone see how they are progressing towards the company target.

PRIZE Half the tickets have 'words of wisdom' written on them, similar to those found on fortune cookies. Of the rest of the tickets, 20% give the chance to select a candy from the candy jar, 20% give the chance to collect a chocolate bar, and 10% are worth a movie ticket or prize of similar value. The grand prize draw is something worth about $100, such as tickets to a special event.

BENEFIT • Helps keep people focused
• Fun and easy competition to run

SOURCE Seamus Martin

2 months

Sales World Cup

A home loan center in a major bank has held the Sales World Cup every year for the past few years. It gains in popularity and success every year and is now a much anticipated event.

PURPOSE
- To maximize sales opportunities in a period that traditionally is regarded as seasonally slow, such as Christmas and New Year

GROUP SIZE 20 to 100 participants, divided into teams of 4 to 10 people

RESOURCE Approximately $30 per team for decorations such as flags or banners

METHOD Divide the sales staff into teams or use the existing teams. Ask each team to come up with a team name to use during the Sales World Cup. Send out an invitation to all staff to participate in the Sales World Cup (see page 145), and include a registration form for all team members to fill out (see page 146). At the bottom of the form there is a clause that says all players agree to participate in the true spirit of the game.

The Sales World Cup starts with 3 preliminary rounds. The objective is to beat the team you are playing against in sales performance and accumulate enough points to compete in the semi-finals. Each round is held over a period of 2 weeks, with each team playing a different team for each 2-week period. A draw at the beginning of the competition will determine which teams compete against each other.

At the end of the 6 weeks the 4 top teams by total accumulation of points compete in two semi-finals. The semi-finals and the final last for a week only. The winners of each semi-final compete in the final. The teams that lost in the semi-finals compete for third and fourth place in the minor final.

The teams compete in 5 events. Each team gains points for each event that it qualifies in. Once the teams have earned qualifying points they can also earn bonus points. For example, the home loan center uses the following types of sales for its 5 events:

1. Conditionally approved home loans
2. Formally approved home loans
3. Conditionally approved home loans linked to a bank account
4. Formally approved home loans linked to a bank account
5. Home loan and investment home loan referrals

The scoring system is as follows:

2 points for meeting the qualifying amount in conditionally approved home loans

2 points for meeting the qualifying amount in conditionally approved home loans linked to a bank account

3 points for meeting the qualifying amount in formally approved home loans

3 points for meeting the qualifying amount in formally approved home loans linked to a bank account

1 point for achieving the qualifying amount in the referral category

7 points for achieving the qualifying amount in all events

1 point each time the team exceeds a qualifying amount by 20% in each event

3 points if victory is achieved over the opposition (if a draw, result points are split)

Teams lose 2 points as a penalty if any player is deemed not to be playing in the spirit of the competition.

A visual scoreboard is updated on a daily basis, which keeps everyone fully informed of the progress of the teams. The sales manager is given the title of President of the Federation of International Sales Association (FISA) for the duration of the game. All disputes or issues are resolved by the President and are final. The President is responsible for sending out invitations, registrations and the notification of winners for each round. At the end of the Sales World Cup the 4 prize winners are awarded their prizes and a morning tea is hosted for all support staff in the sales area.

PRIZE First prize, $100 gift voucher for each team member; second prize, team lunch to the value of $300; third prize, team lunch to the value of $200; fourth prize, 2 movie tickets per team member

BENEFIT • Enhances teamwork and team morale
• Creates a fun and enthusiastic environment
• Keeps people focused and productive during normal slow sales times

SOURCE John Knezevic and Frank Speranza

Sales
World Cup

Congratulations to the

Team name _____

Your team has qualified for
the Sales World Cup.

It is with great pleasure that I
invite you to participate in this
championship event.

Kindly complete the
Team Registration Form

Sales World Cup

Team Registration Form

Team name _____

	Name	Signature	Date
1			
2			
3			
4			
5			
6			
7			
8			
9			
10			
11			
12			

Remember:

By signing this form, team members acknowledge
that they will participate in the true spirit of the game.

4 EFFECTIVE

COMMUNICATION

Communication is a skill that can be improved with constant attention and continual development. The objective of all communication, whether speaking to customers, staff or colleagues, is to achieve a positive response. Included in this section are some games, classroom training exercises and on-the-job training techniques to enhance communication with co-workers and customers.

Top 10 Hits

A team leader wanted to encourage her team members to take more customer service calls without compromising the quality of their communication. To help stimulate this objective she introduced a game that appealed to the interest of her team members. The team members loved music and often burst into a rendition of an outdated and daggy song. She thought that perhaps some type of music game would be a good idea. In a very short time, Top 10 Hits became a top hit with her team.

PURPOSE • To increase the efficient use of time in each customer service call or contact

GROUP SIZE 10 or more people

RESOURCE Corkboard, colored paper, white paper and pins

METHOD Ask each team member to select their all-time favorite song. Print the name of each song and the name of the team member on a white strip of paper that will fit within the width of the corkboard (see page 150). Cover the corkboard with colored paper and decorate the board with a music theme, leaving a special place for the Top 10 Hits list.

Explain to your team that their aim is to make their song reach the Top 10 Hits chart, and their song's place on the chart will depend on their own ranking of performance within the Top 10. The 10 people with the shortest average call time, or who have taken the most calls at the end of the week, will make the Top 10 Hits chart. First place goes to the person with the shortest average call time or the most calls, and everyone else in the Top 10 is ranked accordingly.

At the end of the month, the person with the best average ranking over the 4 weeks becomes the Top 10 Hits performer for the month.

PRIZE Spray a vinyl record with gold paint and place it in a frame. Place the name of the Top 10 Hits performer on the gold record. Present the gold record at a team meeting.

BENEFIT • Helps people to focus in a fun way
        • Inspires people to use games to achieve results in the future

SOURCE Frances Gray

My favorite song

Name

My favorite song

Name

My favorite song

Name

My favorite song

Name

Ongoing, as long as the message is not forgotten that management wants staff's ideas

The Excitement Tray

Staff come up with a lot of great ideas. They may either rush to tell their supervisor, thereby interrupting not only their work but also the supervisor's work, or they may forget the great idea all together. Here is how one team leader managed this challenge.

PURPOSE   • To capture great ideas without interrupting productive time

GROUP SIZE   Any number

RESOURCE   A brightly colored tray on everyone's desk and appreciation certificates (see page 152)

METHOD   Explain to staff that their ideas and enthusiasm are very important. As front-line staff they are in a position to realize what is important to the customer, sales or customer service techniques that work or ways to improve processes.

Explain to them that it is important for them to think of themselves as improvement specialists. Give them each a bright tray and ask them to write down their ideas and place them in the tray. Once a week, you will review their ideas, and ask the team members with really good ideas to present them at the team meeting.

PRIZE   Movie tickets and an appreciation certificate presented in front of colleagues once a month for the best of the best ideas

BENEFIT   • Keeps staff on the phones or in front of customers, instead of jumping up from their desk and telling the team leader every time they come up with a good idea

SOURCE   Anna Marsh-Quigley

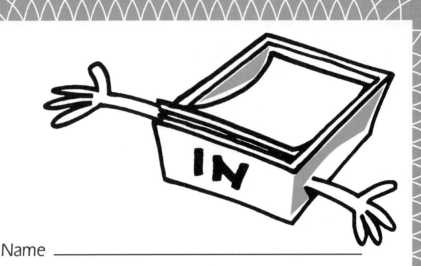

Name _____

IN appreciation of your ideas for improving...

_____

_____

_____

_____

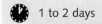

The Slippers of Responsibility

Personality conflicts always seem to boil down to miscommunication and misunderstanding. Such conflicts can usually be fixed with a bit of good humor and by opening up the lines of positive communication. This is a humorous way to communicate to staff that they are expected to get along and resolve any problems that they have.

PURPOSE • To solve personality conflicts in the office

GROUP SIZE Can be used in a large office, but the conflict that is being resolved is between 2 people

RESOURCE 2 pairs of outrageous slippers

METHOD Put on display 2 pairs of large-sized, outrageous slippers. Character slippers are often the best, such as Daffy Duck slippers that quack as you walk or dinosaur slippers that roar.

Tell staff that these are the 'Slippers of Responsibility' and are used to resolve any personality conflicts between people that may occur from time to time in the office.

Those people experiencing conflict will be asked to wear the slippers around the office for a few days until they can resolve their conflict. If they do not solve the conflict by themselves within 2 days, they are guided through their conflict resolution by the 'Slipper Supervisor'. The Slipper Supervisor becomes a rotation position within the office.

REWARD Once the conflict has been resolved by the staff members with or without the help of the Slipper Supervisor, both staff members are rewarded with a brief 'Slipper Removal Ceremony'. This ceremony should be short and fun as the staff members return the slippers to their display position.

BENEFIT • A light-hearted acknowledgment that 2 people have a conflict and are prepared to try and solve the problem
• Gives ownership of the conflict to those involved and their peer group, rather than escalating the problem to management
• Provides an exercise in problem solving

SOURCE Liz Charlesworth

Family and Friends

When a bank's call center required 48 new staff in a hurry, it looked to its existing staff for help. Advertising and using an employment agency were not the only means it could rely on in a competitive marketplace and in the tight time schedule it found itself in. It got the message across very effectively through a campaign designed to encourage staff to help out.

PURPOSE • To recruit staff members quickly and effectively

GROUP SIZE All staff are invited to participate

RESOURCE A memorandum to staff containing job descriptions and qualifications required

METHOD Encourage all staff members to approach and 'sponsor' family and friends who they feel have the capacity and desire to succeed in the office, retail outlet or call center environment.

Give a clear outline of the required qualifications and the recruitment process that each candidate for a job will be asked to go through. For example:
1. submitting a resume
2. preliminary phone interview
3. invitation for an interview in the office
4. 1-hour panel interview and test
5. if successful, offered a position with a 3-month probationary period
6. if unsuccessful, candidates are thanked for their interest in applying
7. if a position is not available, the person can be put on a waiting list for the next recruitment intake

REWARD For each applicant who successfully completes the 3-month probationary period and is offered a full-time position, the sponsor receives a $50 bonus.

BENEFIT • Everyone feels involved
• Sponsors take a special interest in supporting the development and success of the employee they sponsored

SOURCE Graeme Newnham

Quick and Easy Product Training

Product training or procedures training is often done using lectures and overheads. Many people have difficulty with this type of communication. They have trouble paying attention, retaining information and then using the information. This is often because they are passively involved in the communication as listeners. To help people to learn more quickly and get them involved more actively, use this simple but very effective training technique.

PURPOSE • To help people to learn by doing

GROUP SIZE 4 to 24 people

RESOURCE Pamphlets on products or procedures

METHOD Prepare a comprehensive quiz on the knowledge that you would like staff to learn and use—aim for about 20 questions.

Divide the group up into pairs. Tell staff that you are going to hold a competition to see which pair can complete a product or procedures knowledge quiz first. Give each pair all the pamphlets that provide the answers to the quiz and the quiz as well. Give them a time frame that allows just enough time for everyone to finish. As soon as each pair finishes, they are to raise their hands and give the quiz to the facilitator.

Explain that the answers need to be provided with a minimum and maximum number of words. This will prevent lack of thoroughness or answers that are too long. If the participants will need to communicate this information to others as part of their job, it may be preferable to have them write their answers in dialogue form, as they would explain them to customers.

Then have each pair take it in turns to answer a question until all the questions have been discussed. As they answer the question, the others in the group may agree, disagree or provide a better answer.

PRIZE Tell everyone that they are all winners and give candy bars to all as prizes. The objective of the game is not to score right or wrong—participants will continue to learn through discussion.

155

BENEFIT • People learn more easily by talking and doing instead of listening
• A competition adds interest to the learning
• A trainer who is overworked or losing their voice gets to take it easier

SOURCE Victor Greenwich Jr

Create Your Own Game

The creativity and ingenuity of team leaders and staff members alike is amazing when given a few guidelines and a formula for creating a game. As a trainer and presenter, I have used this technique in several workshops. People have a great time and they create clever games that get results.

PURPOSE • To create a game, activity or competition that will produce a specific result. The result may be to increase sales, reduce errors, meet a deadline, reduce stress, improve the quality of customer service or energize the office

GROUP SIZE A team of 3 to 4 people is the best number to create a game

RESOURCE Pen and paper

METHOD **For the game creation**

1. Start with a purpose in mind: what are the results that the game, activity or competition should achieve? Often, a game can achieve more than one result. For example, the purpose of a game could be to increase product knowledge, improve sales performance and reduce absenteeism. How is this possible? Hold a sales game on the day with the most absenteeism and include 3 product knowledge questions as part of the criteria for claiming a prize.

2. Think of a theme that would appeal to most of the people in the office. Are they interested in sports, board games, school days, carnivals, word games, cards, music, travel or food? Is there a special event taking place, such as the World Series Baseball, that you can tie into? Many interests such as board games, sports and cards will give you a structure that you can follow or slightly alter to create your own game. An example is the Sales World Cup activity on pages 142–5.

3. Determine your budget, and in most cases keep it small: $10 for a daily or weekly game or $50 to $100 for a fortnightly or monthly game. The budget includes both resources and prizes. Experience has shown that the smaller the budget, the more creative the game or activity seems to become. Use

the resources you already have around the office or that staff members can bring in easily from home. Prizes can be time off, certificates, coffee or tea made by the team leader or a revolving trophy such a phone painted gold. Large prize money or prize values can work against the outcome. Motivation comes from the fun of playing the game, the competitive element of the activity and the fun of winning.

4. Games can vary in length: they can be for a day, a week, a fortnight or 1 or 2 months. The time frame needs to fit the purpose of the game.

The daily game is ideal:
• for energizing the office
• to launch a new product or service
• to boost production on the busiest day or slowest day each month
• to hold on a day with high absenteeism to encourage people to be there
• as a surprise to show appreciation
• as a way of celebrating a special day, such as St Valentine's Day

The weekly game is ideal:
• to hold after a training day to encourage the implementation of new skills
• at the beginning of the month to get off to a good start
• at the end of the month to help reach or exceed targets
• to help relieve stress and create fun during a hectic week
• to use as an on-the-job training tool during a slow period
• to launch a new product or service

The fortnightly game is ideal:
• to help new staff to get to know their peers and to learn quickly
• to use when a week is too short to meet your game or activity objective
• as a lead-up to a holiday period to help keep staff focused
• to implement a new procedure
• to introduce new product knowledge

The monthly game is ideal:
• when you want to stimulate productivity over a longer

period, by using a series of 4 different weekly games or 2 fortnightly games
- when looking at results on a monthly basis
- because the player dynamics change each week, by creating different teams or different pairs each week
- when you discover a popular game that will hold interest for a month
- when a game or activity is more easily or more fairly scored over a period of a month

5. Games, competitions and activities can be played with any number of people. There are 3 different ways to divide up your group for the game.

Team games work well:
- when a team is striving to reach a specific objective as one unit
- when teams are created to compete against other teams
- when individual competitiveness can create ill feeling
- when you have a range of knowledge and expertise among your staff and you wish this to be shared equally in a team

Pair games work well:
- in small offices
- when you want a less-experienced person to learn from a more-experienced person
- to encourage cooperation between support/administration staff and front-line staff (pair up a support person and a sales person to compete against another pair—often, support staff feel left out of competitions)
- when people feel more comfortable competing in pairs than individually

Individual competitions work well:
- when you have a range of different areas that you can provide competition for, so that the same person does not always win
- when you set a target so that everyone can be a winner
- when you have random winners
- in a sales environment where people are driven to compete
- when people compete against their own past performance

For the game, activity or competition

This is essentially how you are going to play the game. To determine your method consider:

1. using methods found in sports, board games or word games, or any form of competition that would appeal to the people in the office
2. a clear and easy way to score the game
3. how to create fun without disrupting the office
4. the opinion of the players in the office before the game is played

PRIZE Keep the prize value low. The fun should be in playing and winning the game. The prize is just an acknowledgment or something extra that is fun to receive.

BENEFIT • People take ownership when they create their own game
• Allows staff to be creative and innovative

SOURCE Carolyn Greenwich

Productivity Update

Communicating ongoing results to sales people plays a big part in helping everyone to reach their targets. A home lending company used this meeting strategy for very effective results.

PURPOSE
- To insure that everyone is aware of the ongoing performance of their colleagues
- To insure that the manager and team leader are kept up-to-date with progress on a daily basis

GROUP SIZE   4 to 8 team members

RESOURCE   Large whiteboard and colored markers

METHOD   Divide the sales staff into teams unless they are already organized that way. Every month, each team sets its own sales target with the assistance of management. Each team member decides which portion of the team target they will be responsible for achieving. This decision is based on previous performance, hours of work and length of time in the job.

The whiteboard is designed to show the team's target and each individual's target within the team. On the left-hand side, write the name of each team member, with 2 columns next to their name. Head the first column 'Sales achieved to date' and the next 'Sales in progress'.

At the start of the month, hold a 15-minute meeting each week and paste the progress of each team member on the board. Ask each team member to talk about their sales in progress and get tips on how to close the sale from other team members. During the last week of the month, hold meetings each afternoon to help give a boost to productivity.

BENEFIT
- Gives people recognition on a daily basis for their performance
- Makes people realise that it is consistent daily effort that translates into results
- Acts as a subtle form of peer pressure to encourage people to reach their targets

SOURCE   Paul Kennedy

The Ideas Committee

The suggestion box at one company was not working—in fact, the only thing it was getting was complaints! To get constructive feedback and recommendations from staff, the company set up an Ideas Committee. Instead of complaints, the company received valuable time- and money-saving ideas.

PURPOSE • To use the collective intelligence of staff to improve business

GROUP SIZE 6 to 8 people on the committee

RESOURCE A private meeting room and notebook for the minutes

METHOD Select a person or ask for a volunteer from each team or department. The person selected must not be a team leader or supervisor and must take their job on the Ideas Committee seriously.

At each fortnightly meeting, each member brings to the Ideas Committee a recommendation for improvement. This could be an idea for improvements to procedures, competitions, activities, marketing ideas, systems improvements, etc. The Ideas Committee discusses the merits and possibilities of implementing each idea. As a group, it makes a decision to recommend or not to recommend an idea.

The recommendations and the benefits of the idea to the company, staff or customers are sent to the manager. The manager replies to all recommendations after consulting with the various parties who would be affected by the idea.

REWARD The honor and prestige of being a member of the Ideas Committee

BENEFIT • Front-line staff can have a direct link to top management without having their ideas filtered through their team leader or supervisor
• Excellent ideas that might never come to the notice of management are not lost
• All staff feel empowered to put forward workable recommendations through their member on the Ideas Committee

SOURCE Sandra Lau

Lateral Thinkers

A manager of a windscreen company needed his team of customer service representatives to come up with ways to reduce the errors that were being made in deliveries. In order to help create their own solutions, he brought them together for a short course in lateral thinking. This exercise could be used to get staff to help provide solutions for any problem.

PURPOSE • To help staff come up with their own solutions for reducing errors

GROUP SIZE 9 to 24 people

RESOURCE A lateral thinking exercise such as the one below

METHOD Bring your staff together and announce to them that together you all need to come up with some ideas on how to solve a particular problem, such as:
1. a reduction in errors
2. monthly rostering
3. punctuality or absenteeism
4. time management
5. deadlines
6. more effective teamwork
7. provision of timely information

Next, tell them that the best solution is not always obvious. For the next month you would like all of them, working in teams of 3, to think laterally and to come up with a solution that they feel will give the easiest and best result.

Divide the staff into teams of 3 people. Then tell them that to start the ball rolling you are going to present each team with some information followed by a question, which they will need to solve by lateral thinking. The team that guesses the correct answer the fastest will win a prize for each team member.

One at a time, excuse all but one team from the room and present your situation and question to the team. Then start your stopwatch. They are allowed to ask 'yes' or 'no' questions until they come up with an answer. Here is an example of a situation and some questions to ask. (Other questions can be found in a game called 'Mind Trap', which you should find at your local book store or toy store.)

Situation

You are pushing a car. You push it around the corner and come to a hotel, but you know you cannot go in because you are broke.

Questions

What are you doing?
What is the situation?

Answer

You are playing a game of monopoly! The car is the monopoly car, the hotel is one of the hotels on the monopoly board, and you cannot go into the hotel because you have no more monopoly money.

After each team has been timed, invite all the teams back into the meeting room to announce the winners.

Then ask each of the teams to come up with a solution to the original problem, which they will be asked to present at the next team meeting in a month's time. The best idea will be selected and implemented.

PRIZE   A bottle of wine for each member of the winning team that comes up with the best way to solve the problem

BENEFIT
- Staff enjoy and appreciate the novelty of team meetings
- Staff take ownership when they solve problems themselves

SOURCE   Gary Street

The Quiz Show

Helping people to learn and understand products and procedures is always a challenge. This game will help people after a training session, or after they have been given information to study and read. The game will help them reinforce and retain the important information.

PURPOSE
- To help people to learn and remember important information

GROUP SIZE 5 to 8 people, divided into teams

RESOURCE Note cards and whiteboard to keep score

METHOD Divide the group into 2 to 3 teams. Give each team 15 note cards and written information on the subject they are to be quizzed about. Ask them to come up with 15 questions and answers about the subject. Provide 4 categories of question to be asked and allocate points to each category, such as:

4 general knowledge questions	1 point if answered correctly
6 in-depth questions	2 points if answered correctly
3 situation questions (i.e. if this happened, what would be the best solution)	3 points, or partial points, if answered correctly
2 obscure questions	4 points if answered correctly

Ask the teams to write the category of question at the top of each card. Give them 10 to 15 minutes to come up with their questions and send them off into different areas of the room. Ensure that each team writes its team name on its card so that it is not asked those questions. Then invite everyone back into the game area and collect the question and answer cards. The training facilitator, team leader or manager acts as the game host, and asks the question and places the score on the whiteboard.

Each team sits around a table. One chair is provided in front of the table for the person who is answering the question. Each person takes a turn at answering the questions and is required to sit in the chair. They can turn around to ask for help from their team, but they must decide on and give the final answer within 1 minute.

The teams draw to see who starts first. The game host asks the first team a question, writes up the score and then asks the next team a question. If the question has been asked before, it can be asked again or replaced with a question provided by the game host.

When all questions have been asked, the team with the most points wins.

PRIZE   Chocolates for the winning team; bubblegum for the losing team

BENEFIT • Easy learning through involvement and competition

SOURCE   Lucie Booker

The Tissue Box

This is a fun, easy icebreaker or getting-to-know-you game. For the very brave, it can also be done with a roll of toilet paper.

PURPOSE
- To introduce a new group of people to each other
- To get people who already work together to get to know each other better

GROUP SIZE 6 to 12 people

RESOURCE A box of tissues

METHOD At the beginning of a training session or team meeting, the session leader enters the room with a box of tissues. They say to the group, 'My name is ...., and when I have a cold I use 5 tissues to blow my nose each hour', and then take that number of tissues from the box. They throw the box of tissues to someone in the room and ask that person how many tissues they use an hour when they have a cold. That person is asked to tell the group and then to take that number of tissues from the box. The box is then thrown back to the session leader, who keeps throwing it to each person in the group.

Once everyone has finished, the session leader then says to the group: 'For each tissue you have taken from the box, I would like you to tell us something about yourself.' If someone has been funny and has taken lots of tissues from the box, they will soon discover that the last laugh is on them. If the group members already know each other, ask them to tell the group things about themselves that most people do not know. Everyone is given a few minutes to write down or think about what they will tell the group about themselves, such as:
1. their favorite color, food, pet or city
2. the number of brothers and sisters they have or perhaps their birth order
3. their previous work experience

When everyone has had their turn, the seminar leader takes their turn, but tells the group about 5 things that they will cover in the meeting or 5 things that they will learn in the session.

BENEFIT • Helps people to prepare for learning by involving them immediately

SOURCE Lindall Duffy

Energizing Customer Service

An energy company used this activity to help its customer service representatives to focus on providing excellence in customer service. The company called this activity 'Energizing Customer Service' to tie in with its industry. A retail outlet, branch office or department could adapt this activity easily to improve communication.

PURPOSE
• To help people concentrate on their communication skills and use customer service language

GROUP SIZE
Any number of people

RESOURCE
A brightly decorated box for the 'Energizing Customer Service' forms (see page 171)

METHOD
Most customer service people are trained to use language that customers will respond to positively. Make a list of the parts of a conversation with a customer that you feel are important for the customer service person to use well. This may include:
1. the greeting
2. using the customer's name
3. using the words 'thank you'
4. asking appropriate questions
5. presenting information in a clear and concise manner
6. acknowledging what is important to the customer
7. a customer satisfaction question or a closing question
8. saying goodbye to the customer

Managers or team leaders hear staff speaking to customers on the phone or in person every day. When you hear a staff member speaking extremely well to a customer using the language that is expected of them, write down on the Energizing Customer Service form what the staff member said that impressed you and then sign it. Hand this form to the staff member with positive comments about what you have heard. The staff member then puts the form in the box for the monthly draw. The more of these forms the staff member collects, the more chances they have to win the monthly prize. At the end of the month, one form is drawn from the box.

PRIZE $50 gift voucher

BENEFIT • Helps people to stay focused over time
          • Gives instant reward and appreciation

SOURCE Terri–Lee Duffy

Thank you

_____

for energizing customer service

I was impressed by your customer service
communication when

_____

_____

_____

_____

_____

_____

Signed _____

Did I Say?

Often, people are unaware how they sound to their co-workers or customers. This activity will make people think of what type of impact their communication has on other people.

PURPOSE
- To help people to think before they speak and, as a result, improve their communication skills
- To help people to realize the value of working in a team

GROUP SIZE 8 to 30 people

RESOURCE Newspapers

METHOD Give each person in the group a newspaper and ask them to make an object with the paper. When they have finished making their objects, ask them to find a partner with whom to play 'Show and Tell'. One person starts by showing their object to their partner and asking 'What is it?' Then the other person in the pair does the same.

When everyone has had a chance to show their object to their partner, ask for the group's attention. Ask the group how many of them thought or may have even said, 'That doesn't look much like a...', 'I could have done better' or 'You call that a ...?' Gently ask them if they would say such things to a child. If so, what do they think the child's reaction might be? And if this attitude continued over a period of time, what might be the end result? People from the group may possibly say that they might shut down or stop trying for fear of ridicule, not being accepted or being embarrassed. Ask them if this has ever happened to them in the workplace or if they feel they were ever guilty of discouraging another person at the office.

After this has been discussed and the answers are leading towards listening and caring for their fellow workers, ask 'Did I say you had to make an object on your own? Did anyone think of using anything that was within reach to add to their object?' After listening to the answers, ask 'How much more could have been done if this had been a team effort?' and discuss their answers.

BENEFIT • Promotes the importance of teamwork
         • Allows childhood play and fun
         • Helps people rethink what they say and do

SOURCE Benita Collings

Heart and Soul

Everyone loves to be thought highly of. Often, people do not have the opportunity to let others know that they admire and respect certain qualities about them. This simple activity can do wonders to build self-esteem and mutual respect within a team or a group.

PURPOSE
• To provide an opportunity for people to give positive feedback to others in their team

GROUP SIZE
8 to 19 people (split larger groups into groups of 8 to 10 people)

RESOURCE
A sheet of paper for each participant (see page 176)

METHOD
Version 1

At the end of a training day, provide everyone with a sheet of paper (or a page at the end of a workbook), at the top of which there is a blank space. Ask everyone to write their name in this space. Underneath this space is the following instruction: Please write down positive comments about this person from a professional standpoint, which describe what you have admired, appreciated or respected about this person during the course of the training period.

Ask each person to pass the paper with their name on it clockwise around the table, so that everyone can write a positive comment about them on the sheet.

When the sheet returns to the original person, give everyone time to read what others have written about them.

Version 2

To keep what has been written confidential, ask everyone to start their comments at the bottom of the page. After they have written their comment, they simply fold the paper over to keep their comment private. Then they pass the paper around the group until everyone has had an opportunity to write a comment.

BENEFIT   • Makes people feel good as they read the positive things that
            colleagues have said about them

SOURCE   Carolyn Greenwich and Muffy McWhinnie

HEART AND SOUL

Name _____

Please write down positive comments about this person from a professional standpoint, which describe what you have admired, appreciated or respected about this person during the course of the training period.

_____

_____

_____

_____

_____

_____

_____

_____

Doctor of the Discontented

One of the most difficult challenges in communication is to remain calm when confronted with a complaint by a customer or fellow staff member. This simple visual exercise will help almost anyone to reduce their defensive responses when confronted with this type of difficult and often emotional situation.

PURPOSE
- To help people to learn through role-plays how to respond in an effective, constructive and caring manner when confronted with an irate customer or angry fellow staff member

GROUP SIZE 4 to 20 people

RESOURCE White jacket

METHOD Ask for 2 volunteers to 'play doctor' in front of the group. One person will be the patient consulting the doctor and the other will play the caring and concerned doctor. Ask the person who is playing doctor to wear a doctor's white lab coat.

Set up the 'doctor–patient' scenario. Suggest that the person playing the doctor behave like their family doctor. The patient can come up with any type of ailment that is non-controversial. Ask the person role-playing the doctor to listen intently, give acknowledgment by nodding and using vocal expressions, and express empathy and desire to help with the problem. The role-play finishes when some sort of resolution has taken place.

Now ask the same volunteers to change the scenario to a common customer complaint situation. This situation can be suggested by the facilitator or the group. Ask them to role-play as before, with the doctor playing the company representative role while still wearing the white doctor's coat. The patient becomes the customer. Ask the company representative to continue thinking and acting like a 'doctor' in their responses. Explain that this will help keep them from being defensive, and will focus them on being empathic and helpful to the customer.

Ask the observers in the group to select a role-play partner and repeat the role-plays that they have observed. Once they have completed these role-plays, ask them to change roles so that everyone has an opportunity to play both the doctor and the patient and the company representative and the customer.

When all the role-plays have been completed, ask the group to come up with 5 actions they have learned from the exercise that they will definitely use next time they are in the same situation to achieve better results. They may come up with:

1. be empathic, but remain detached
2. listen actively by acknowledging the person's concerns
3. take a rational not emotional approach to complaints
4. fight the urge to become defensive
5. show confidence by taking control and providing a resolution

BENEFIT
- The analogy of the 'Doctor of the Discontented' gives people a new prescription for handling complaints
- Lots of fun and laughter makes learning more effective
- The message is demonstrated more easily by the involvement of participants

SOURCE Muffy McWhinnie

Birth Order

People are always most curious to learn more about themselves. Often, they wonder why they think or act like some people and yet are so different from others. This exercise will help everyone in the group to relate to and communicate with other people in the organization from a new perspective.

PURPOSE • To let people learn how their birth order may affect their communication style

GROUP SIZE 12 to 40 people

RESOURCE Handout provided (see page 182)

METHOD 1. Explain to the group that birth order may influence how we all communicate and relate to other people. Tell them that you are going to read out generalized descriptions of people based on birth order. Then, to understand how this may impact in the workplace, you are going to divide them into groups of the same birth order for a structured discussion.

2. Ask all those who are the oldest child in their family to raise their hands. Then read the following to them:

   As the first born, it is generally felt that you are a total over-achiever. Nothing slows you down, least of all an obstacle. The greater the challenge, the more determined you become. You never think twice about fighting for what you want. You have a tendency to be very serious and overly responsible. Having helped younger brothers or sisters, you are good at nurturing and supporting others. As a result of your birth order, you often feel more at ease with people who are a lot older or much younger than yourself. On the whole, you are organized and methodical.

   On the negative side, you can be a perfectionist. As a child you may have ripped up your homework if there was one error in it and started over. Sometimes, you find it hard to say that you do not know something or to say 'no' to more responsibility. This is because you do not want anyone to know that you are not perfect.

3. Now ask for a show of hands from those who are middle children. Then read the following to them:

   Often, as a middle child you take great pride in being a rebel and in being different. At the same time, as a middle child you have learned the skill of being a peacemaker. You are a good negotiator, a great listener and sensitive to others. You deal well with all ages, and people describe you as open-minded and patient with others.

Generally, you are described as a great socialiser. You know just how to win friends and influence people. Walking into a room full of people, known and unknown, is not a problem for you. While your competitive nature is a strength, your weakness can often be becoming overly competitive or aggressive. Often, this need to constantly compete reveals an insecurity within you.

4. Next, ask those who are the youngest child to raise their hands. Then read the following to them:

Generally, you expect attention because you have received it your entire life. You may have been the class clown in school. You are fun-loving, affectionate and have a great sense of humor. Many of you may feel that you are not taken seriously, and you can become overly-assertive. On the negative side, you almost always need to have the last word. You hate to be told you are wrong and also know where to hit people where they are most vulnerable.

5. Lastly, ask the only children to raise their hands. Then read the following to them:

As an only child, you often are very confident and extremely responsible. Having been number one most of your life, you have no desire to change this status. As a result, you talk yourself into becoming an expert in the areas where you can easily shine. You are innovative and daring, sophisticated and independent. Many would call you extremely conscientious and reliable. On the negative side, you could be described as self-centered, set in your ways and a loner.

6. Having given every group this generalized description of their birth order, ask everyone to form a group with others of the same birth order. Tell the groups that they may or may not agree with the description of the personality traits of their birth order. It is their objective to have a group discussion to come up with common communication characteristics that they all share. Each group will need to appoint a group leader and a scribe to take notes. In their discussions they need to answer the following questions:

   • What 4 communication characteristics help you achieve a positive response? Provide an actual example for each communication characteristic.

   • What 4 communication characteristics would you describe as your most troublesome? Provide an actual example for each communication characteristic.

   Depending on the size of the groups, allow 10 to 15 minutes for the discussion. Ask each group to stand up and give its findings to the other groups. Conclude by explaining the benefits of this type of exercise, as follows:

BENEFIT
- Helps people to understand what their strengths are in communication and what changes they may need to make
- Helps people to bond with others of the same birth order in their group
- Helps people to understand that their difficulties with communication are shared by others

SOURCE Carolyn Greenwich

Birth Order

Question 1   What 4 communication characteristics help you achieve a positive response?
Provide an actual example for each communication characteristic.

Question 2   What 4 communication characteristics would you describe as your most troublesome?
Provide an actual example for each communication characteristic.

Clear or Confused?

Customer service, help desk or telesales representatives often need to make a complex issue easily understood. A call center manager used this exercise and it helped everyone to realize that communication is not as easy as it seems.

PURPOSE
• To help people understand that, unless they think carefully about the words, phrases and sequence of information that they provide, they may confuse customers

GROUP SIZE 8 to 12 people

RESOURCE Partition, paper and colored pens

METHOD The facilitator prepares in advance a picture that they have drawn on a piece of A4 paper using 4 different colored pens. The picture can be of any subject or style that they wish.

The group is then divided into group A and group B. The members of each group are asked to sit together on either side of a partition so that they cannot see the other group.

The facilitator puts the picture up on the partition facing group A. Group A is instructed to describe the picture to group B so that they can duplicate the picture as closely as possible. All communication must be verbal. Group A can give any type of description it likes. The group chooses one person to be the spokesperson, while the other members of the group plan and assist how the picture should be described. Group B can ask for any type of clarification it feels that it needs, and will probably choose to have one person draw the picture for the group.

The groups are given no more than 20 minutes for this exercise. At the end of 20 minutes, both pictures are taken down, the partition is removed and the results are shown to the assembled group.

To debrief the members of group A, the facilitator should:
1. Ask how they felt when they saw the picture that group B had drawn.
2. Ask what communication they felt might have caused confusion and what communication they felt was very clear.

3. Ask the group leader whether they felt the whole group was supporting them or whether they felt left on their own to come up with the solution.

Then the facilitator should ask the members of group B:

1. What communication they felt was very clear and what communication they felt was very confusing.

2. How they would have liked the picture described to them so that they could draw it more clearly.

The facilitator should then ask for a summation from the whole group on 3 ways to make sure that communication is clear, and 3 things to avoid so as not to confuse the listener.

BENEFIT
- Helps people to realise how someone feels when they are trying to learn a new concept over the phone
- Helps people to be more patient and emphatic when explaining a concept to the customer
- Reinforces the need to support and help each other in a team to find the best and clearest way to communicate to customers

SOURCE Sherri Prior

Sale of the Century

Helping people to retain important knowledge can be made easier by using team competition as part of a training session. This is a quick and simple game that helps make learning and communicating new facts and information much easier. This game is based on a popular TV game show called 'Sale of the Century'.

PURPOSE
- To make learning fun and easy
- To help people to remember important information that is necessary for communication with customers

GROUP SIZE
2 to 4 people is ideal (for larger groups, play the game 3 times and have a play-off with the 3 winners—more questions will need to be prepared)

RESOURCE
Buzzer or bell for each participant

METHOD
Prepare questions in advance on the products, services and procedures that are covered in training. You may also include some general knowledge questions if you need more questions for more games.

Explain to all the participants that they will be playing against each other. The person who has the highest points at the end of the 3 rounds is declared the winner and collects the prize. Use buzzers such as those found in the 'Sale of the Century' board game. Each person has their own buzzer and wins points for each question that they answer correctly. The first person to hit the buzzer gets to answer the question. If they answer incorrectly, points are deducted. Each answer is worth 5 points if correct and minus 5 points if incorrect.

The rounds are as follows:
Round 1   5 questions of varying difficulty
Round 2   10 quick questions, again of varying difficulty
Round 3   5 questions of a higher degree of difficulty
The person with the highest score at the end of the game is the winner.

PRIZE Any popular item under the value of $5

BENEFIT • Helps identify areas of weakness for future training
• Brings an up–beat ending to a day of training
• Encourages people to pay attention during training, knowing that they will be playing a game at the end of the day

SOURCE Elizabeth Lawther

The Zoo Game

This is sure to liven up a training session and get people out of their comfort level. At the same time, the participants will hopefully learn something about communication.

PURPOSE
• A communication game to help people experience the different perceptions we all have and how this may affect the way we communicate

GROUP SIZE   20 people

RESOURCE   Pieces of paper containing the names of various animals

METHOD   Give all participants a piece of paper with the name of an animal on it and tell them that they are not to reveal the name of the animal to anyone. Then give everyone a blindfold. Ask them to space themselves out around the room and then put their blindfolds on. Once their blindfolds are on, they are to repeatedly make the sound of the animal that they have been assigned. By listening for the same animal sound, they are to find the other animals of their type and form a group. Play until all the people have found a group.

Assign 4 animal types, 1 that is easy to mimic and 3 that are more difficult, for example:
1. a duck
2. a monkey
3. a lion
4. a horse

Make sure that the room is clear of obstacles so no one runs into anything. Ask a couple of people to volunteer not to play, so that they can help people not to run into walls or chairs.

At the completion of the game nearly everyone will be laughing. Ask each group to give an example of the different sounds that were made in their group for the same animal.

Make the point that different tones and words may have different meanings to different listeners. As communicators, it is important to be aware of this in order to be clearly understood.

PRIZE For the team that finishes first, award a packet of animal crackers biscuits.

BENEFIT • Great as an icebreaker, an energizer or just for plain fun

SOURCE Sherri Prior

The 'I Appreciate You' Award

To give staff and management a constructive way to communicate appreciation to each other, and to encourage teamwork, positive attitudes and a more productive atmosphere, this easy system was put in place by a direct marketing wine company. It was so successful that the company used it for a whole year.

PURPOSE • To encourage people to appreciate and value the contributions of others within the organization

GROUP SIZE 50 to 200 participants

RESOURCE Appreciation certificates

METHOD Provide each staff member with a set of appreciation certificates (see page 191). Any time the staff value the contribution of another person within the organization, regardless of that person's position or department, they are able to award them with an 'I Appreciate You' certificate, which shows the specific action that they value in the person that they are rewarding. Such actions might be something that has benefited the person giving the award, the company or a customer. For example:

1. helping on a specific project
2. handling a difficult issue
3. providing excellent customer service
4. working late
5. exceeding targets
6. sharing information
7. educating the person in a specific area
8. making a cup of coffee for them
9. boosting the spirits of the team
10. suggesting a time-saving idea

The original certificate is given to the person appreciated and a copy is given to the team that decides the monthly winner (this team does not participate in the giving or receiving of awards). At the end of the month, the judging team meets to review all the awards and to decide on the overall monthly winner, based on the volume and type of awards that everyone has received. Staff who receive a number of certificates are also acknowledged.

PRIZE $50 gift certificate for the winner and a monthly appreciation award

BENEFIT • Provides positive feedback from peers, departments and management to staff and from staff to management
         • Gives people outside the sales arena a chance to receive appreciation and recognition

SOURCE   Julianne Wargren

Three Cheers for

_____

I greatly appreciate

_____

_____

_____

_____

Thank you

Signed _____

Top 10 Worst Speech Practices

Poor speech habits can impact on the ability of staff to project a professional image of themselves and the organization that they represent. With this month-long activity the use of negative words and phrases such as 'sorry', 'can't', 'you've lost me' and 'no worries' declines dramatically.

PURPOSE • To help staff to become aware of their speech and how the use of certain words and phrases can impact on the outcome of conversations with customers

GROUP SIZE 10 to 14 people

RESOURCE Large poster, paper and big felt pens

METHOD Introduce the 'Top 10 Worst Speech Practices' at a team meeting. Tell the staff that we are not always aware of the jargon, slang or negative words or phrases that we use because we do not hear ourselves. To help everyone become more aware of negative language, ask them to come up with what they consider to be the 'Top 10 Worst Speech Practices'. Once they have agreed on the Top 10, discuss the alternatives to these words or phrases. For example, instead of 'no worries', encourage staff to say 'thank you' or 'you're welcome'.

Ask staff to create a poster highlighting the 'Top 10 Worst Speech Practices' and display the poster in the team area.

Next, ask the team members to pair up with one another. Their job is to listen to each other and tally the number of times they hear the other person use one of the 'Top 10 Worst Speech Practices'. Provide a sheet of paper with the list so they can easily mark them against the sheet.

Team members will have plenty of laughs when they are caught out or catch their partner using the one of the Top 10.

At a weekly team meeting, ask everyone to report how many times they were caught using the words or phrases. Ask each person what they could have said that would have improved the communication. Also ask the team members if they heard any other phrases that they feel should be avoided.

Each week, provide the person who used the least negative words with a small prize.

PRIZE   A box of chocolates, bottle of wine or a movie ticket

SOURCE   Andrew Carr

Paper Trading

People learn most easily by involvement and personal experience. The training manager of a large stock brokerage devised an ongoing learning game that lasted for the period of the 4-week induction program. This helped the new customer service representatives to learn about the stock market and the emotions of the investors that they would be dealing with.

PURPOSE
• To give people new to the finance industry a feeling of involvement in the particular market that they are entering. This can be used by companies in the stock market, managed funds, options or other types of investment products

GROUP SIZE 10 to 15 people

RESOURCE Copies of the company's new account forms

METHOD During the first week of training, give new staff the forms to establish a trading account, just as you would give to a new client. Give them a fictitious voucher for $10 000 to invest. Ask them to make their own investment decisions based on their own research and investment strategies. When they are placing a trade, they have to work out the total cost of the trade, including the cost of the shares and the trade costs such as brokerage, fees or taxes that will be incurred. Provide the participants with dummy contract notes or transaction confirmations.

Encourage the participants to monitor their investments for a 4-week period, using charts and performance figures. They may change their portfolios as often as they wish. All trade costs are to be calculated and deducted along the way.

Each week, hold a discussion for everyone to review their portfolio. At the end the period, debrief the exercise by asking the individuals what they have learned about investing. Encourage them to discuss their observations and feelings.

PRIZE Give a $5 to $10 gift to the person with the best performing portfolio.

BENEFIT   • Gets people actively reading about and discussing stocks
           • Helps participants to learn the associated costs of a trade
           • Creates a fun and friendly competition

SOURCE   Sally Wares

The Learn by Doing Race

The object of this game is to increase staff confidence in using cross-selling communication. This is done saturation style—the more they use it, the easier it becomes. As staff grow more confident, sales increase.

PURPOSE • To help people to focus on cross-selling communication when they speak to customers

GROUP SIZE 5 to 20 people

RESOURCE Whiteboard and pens or corkboard and colored paper

METHOD Draw a racetrack on the whiteboard or, for better effect, use green paper on the corkboard. The drawing of the track can represent any distance you choose for the race. Give each person a horse with their name on it (see page 198).

Every time a staff member uses a cross-selling phrase, their horse moves forward. For example, if the track represents 3200 meters, each time they use a cross-selling phrase they would move a distance of 20 meters. On the track, draw a hurdle every 200 meters. To jump the hurdle staff need to achieve a sale. Sales may be obtained at any time, and can be held to jump other hurdles.

The winner of the race is the first horse past the post. To win, staff need to achieve at least 16 sales and ask cross-selling questions on 160 occasions. This gives a lot of practice of sales language.

As the race progresses the sales manager should walk around to encourage and listen to staff cross-selling. Staff use the honor system to mark down each time they use a cross-selling phrase. At regular intervals throughout the day the manager marks each staff member's progress on the racetrack.

For a 1-day competition the course can be shortened and for a week's competition the course can be lengthened.

PRIZE Have a first, second and third place prize and a random prize draw for anyone who finishes the race in the allotted time.

Keep the total prize value within $100 (i.e. $40 for first prize, $30 for second prize and $15 for third prize and the random draw).

BENEFIT
- Helps people to implement cross-selling after training
- Helps people to focus on the simple language that achieves sales

SOURCE   Wayne Lewin

Training Icebreakers

An experienced trainer found these 2 icebreakers very effective in creating a relaxed, happy and productive atmosphere that fostered learning and encouraged interaction in training sessions.

PURPOSE • To encourage people to interact and to create fun and humor

Icebreaker 1: Learning Pursuit

GROUP SIZE 20 to 160

 15 to 30 minutes

RESOURCE Small note cards for each participant, half in one color and half in another color

METHOD Pick a topic or topics that most people in the group have an interest in or are familiar with. Use one set of colored cards to write the questions on, such as 'Which actress starred in *Cleopatra*?' Each card should contain a different question and the questions should not be too hard.

On the other colored cards write the answers to the questions. Give each person a card as they walk in. Ask them not to look at the card until everyone has been given a card.

Now explain to the assembled group that they are to find the person who has the answer to their question or the question to their answer. People will then start to circulate around the room talking and laughing with each other. Ask people to sit down with their 'match' once they have found them. When everyone has sat down, welcome them to the session.

PRIZE If you wish to give a prize, ask each person to write their name on the card and then place these in a box for a random draw.

BENEFIT • Fun and laughter
• Creates a relaxed start to the training session

Icebreaker 2: Humor Break

GROUP SIZE   8 to 10 people

 5-minute interval four times during a training session

RESOURCE   A4 sheet of paper for each participant

METHOD   The facilitator asks each person to write on one side of the paper, 'What I would do if', then asks them to complete the phrase with an embarrassing or challenging situation. They are only to pose the situation, not give the answer or solution. For example, they could write: 'What I would do if I came to work wearing non-matching shoes.'

They then fold the paper in half and in half again, put their initials on one of the outside corners and give the folded paper to the facilitator. The facilitator redistributes the papers to the others in the group, making sure that no one receives back their own paper. Without looking at the contents, the person writes the answer to their own original problem on the outside of the new paper that they are given.

The facilitator collects the folded papers again and at four intervals throughout the day, stops to read a few at a time. They will usually bring humorous results, as the solutions to the problems are so ridiculous. For example, one problem might be, 'What I would do if a customer has experienced really bad service and has called me to complain', and the answer might be, 'I would go home and change my shoes' (which is the solution to the earlier question, 'What I would do if I came to work wearing non-matching shoes').

PRIZE   The group votes on the most ridiculous problem and solution for the day and the 2 contributors win a candy bar.

BENEFIT   • Fun and laughter
   • Gives a chance to relax during training

SOURCE   John McCoy-Lancaster

List of Contributors

Carolyn Adams, David Johnson, Paula Luethen, Ann-Marie Catlin and Kate McKechnie comprise the management team of Bank SA Telebanking. The team has managed an award-winning call center since 1998. During this time, the call center and the organization have undergone significant changes. The call center has increased from 63 to 160 seats. Employee surveys report that staff are committed, and feel that their opinions are valued and that the company is serious about improving work organization. Attrition rates have been maintained well below industry standards.

Raz Babic has had a 15-year career in banking. She worked at the branch level for several years before progressing to a training role in personal banking. Raz then moved to the customer service call center as a Service Team Leader and was then promoted to a Team Leader of Sales. She is currently enjoying a career break raising her young son, Jacob.

Hamish Bamford is currently the Commercial Manager, Tasman, for Australia–New Zealand Direct Line (ANZDL). ANZDL is a shipping line that transports cargo between Australia, New Zealand, the Islands and North America. Hamish's responsibilities include revenue and cost management for the service to New Zealand. In the 12 years that Hamish has worked for ANZDL, he has held various positions within the company, including Inside Sales Manager, Marketing Manager, and Quality and Training Manager. Hamish holds a Bachelor of Business Studies in Marketing from Massey University, New Zealand. ANZDL obtained the Australian Quality Award for Business Excellence in 1998. Quality management principles underpin ANZDL's approach to running a business and are a significant part of the company's overall success. The company views its staff as one of its key customers and recognition of their efforts is very important. The 'Check You Out' program proves to be very successful in motivating staff. It is a simple system that allows staff at all levels to recognize the performance excellence of other staff. It is one part of several levels of recognition that the company uses.

John Barry is a consultant for the call center industry. He joined Coolong Connections in May 1997 with more than 7 years experience working in and with telephone-based operations. While John's focus has been on managing people to achieve performance improvement, he has developed a solid foundation in call center telephone and information systems. John established the Optus Vision call center in Brisbane, where he demonstrated an ability to achieve high levels of quality sales and service, while addressing key productivity, technology and measurement issues. Working with business statistics, John developed ways to measure service quality results, balancing measures focusing on volumes and activity.

Lucie Booker is a training consultant and facilitator who develops customized customer service and sales training programs. She favors an experiential approach to training, drawing together her extensive training experience and acting background to insure the learning is accessible to all participants. Lucie has developed and delivered a variety of training programs to the call center industry, including team leadership, inbound and outbound sales, time management, coaching, and database and software training. Lucie can be contacted by e-mail at *lucieb@mira.net*.

Andrew Carr commenced in Bank SA's call center in 1992, where he worked as a Sales Consultant in the inbound sales unit. In 1996, Andrew was seconded to establish Bank SA's telemarketing unit, and following the secondment was appointed Team Leader of the inbound sales unit. From 1996 to 1999, Andrew worked as a Team Leader of both the inbound sales and telemarketing units, until being appointed as Manager, Residential and Outbound Sales in October 1999. Andrew's success as Team Leader was recognized through the Australian Teleservices Association Team Leader of the Year Award in 1998. When asked what he likes best about his role, Andrew says, 'I get a great deal of satisfaction from seeing other people learn and develop and go on to achieve levels of performance that they previously felt they would never achieve'.

Margaret Casey is a specialist call center consultant with the design and application of human resource methodologies, profit center/outbound integration and call center audits. Margaret's expertise in call centers has been derived from over 18 years across diverse industries, including telecommunications, financial services, insurance, advertising, media, transport and recruitment. Margaret has presented and facilitated workshops in Asia on the world's best practice in human resource methodologies, outbound strategies, performance measures and call center improvements. Margaret can be contacted by e-mail at *mcasey@ie.net.au*.

Liz Charlesworth has worked for the Australian Teleservices Association, the Australian call center industry association. In her management role, she organized industry events, training programs and sponsorship. She has a passion for the call center industry within Australia and the exciting developments ahead. Liz is currently Marketing Communications Manager for *TelCall Magazine*, the magazine of the Australian Teleservices Association.

Kris Cole is an industrial psychologist and manufacturing technologist. For the past few years, Kris has worked with leading organizations to help strengthen their most persuasive competitive asset, their people. Kris specializes in management and executive development, building powerfully effective work teams, productivity management, communication and organizational change. Kris's management books, *Crystal Clear Communication* and *Supervision and Management in Action*, have been translated into four languages. For more information on Kris's management consultancy, Bax Associates, see their Web site at *http://www.bax.com.au*.

Benita Collings is a speaker/trainer and dynamic media personality with 30 years experience in radio, stage, TV and film. Her sessions make use of a wide range of motivational skills, including generative learning, neurolinguistic programming and theatresports, to create enhanced communication, higher productivity and profits. Benita is also the past president of the National Speakers Association of Australia. Benita can be reached by e-mail at *benitacollings@hotmail.com*.

Cheryl Dooley was a pioneer of business-to-business call centers in Australia. She established her first call center in 1980 and subsequently established and managed 4 call centers in the IT and transport industries before starting her own business, Dooley Dynamics, in 1990. Dooley Dynamics Pty Ltd is now one of the leading consulting and training organizations in the industry and Cheryl has worked widely throughout Australia and Asia on both consulting and training projects. Cheryl has authored two books, *Telemarketing* and *Telephone Techniques*. The Pan Pacific Direct Marketing Symposium made Cheryl its Marketing Excellence Achiever in 1994.

Stephen Dooley has spent his whole working life in the technology arena, from guided missiles to computer networks to telephone systems. He has written call center software for companies in Asia and Australia. He established his first call center in 1989 before joining Dooley Dynamics in 1992. Dooley Dynamics has worked with IBM Asia Pacific to establish call centers from India to Japan. Stephen spent 12 months living in China working to establish IBM's database marketing there. Stephen is often published in industry magazines. Stephen is the General Manager of Dooley Dynamics and is considered the company's database and technical expert.

Lindall Duffy is a financial analyst with the Sydney Organizing Committee of the Olympic Games (SOCOG). She works in the precincts and venues division of the organization. Prior to joining SOCOG, Lindall worked for local government as a trainee accountant. She has completed a Bachelor of Business at Charles Sturt University and is currently studying part-time a Diploma of Personnel Management.

Terri-Lee Duffy is the Recruitment and Training Manager for Energy Australia's call center. Prior to joining Energy Australia, Terri-Lee spent 7 years at Ansett Airlines Australia in various call center positions. Terri-Lee has project-managed the relocation of the Energy Australia Sydney call center and the realignment of workforce management processes.

Kym Eveleigh is currently the Inbound Call Center and Training Manager for Australian Wine Selectors (AWS). Since commencing with AWS in 1997 as a Sales and Motivation Supervisor, Kym has seen the call center more than treble in size and move from a totally manual operation into a leading edge high-tech environment. Commencing work as a fitter and turner, Kym moved into engineering sales. From there she entered the call center industry, working as a telemarketer with CIG Insurance before moving to AWS. Kym is passionate about call center sales and service and is constantly developing new strategies for motivating staff to achieve and exceed customers' expectations.

Jann Fenley has worked in the financial industry for over 30 years. For the last 10 years she has worked for the Police Credit Union and is currently Manager for Direct Operations. Jann has built her success as a manager by keeping her staff motivated and enthusiastic. To achieve this, Jann uses a variety of incentives, games and competitions. Results speak for themselves, as her team meets and exceeds its targets on a regular basis. She believes that the best activities reward not only the best performer, but also the most improved and those that try hardest. Jann encourages her team members to set their own targets and develop their own reward schemes.

Tracey Flynn is Head of Investor Services for Colonial First State. Tracey is responsible for all interactions with investors, including telephone, written and e-mail communication. Tracey has worked in various customer service roles in the financial service industry for the last 12 years. In 1999, Tracey was named Call Center Manager of the Year for New South Wales, in recognition of her achievements attained through changes implemented within the call center. Tracey believes that dealing with change is the most challenging and rewarding aspect of her career. She feels fortunate to be part of the dynamic call center industry.

Louise Fritschy started her career in sales in 1993 and was quickly appointed to the position of Sales and Marketing Manager with Airnorth. With her considerable success in corporate sales, Louise joined Hertz Australia as Business Center Manager. Her role was to help set up and grow a new sales channel for Hertz. In all her positions, Louise has gained considerable hands-on experience in recruitment, training, sales marketing and planning. Louise took a break from corporate life to start a family and has recently re-entered the work force on a part-time basis for Has Solutions, as a Client Support Officer.

Manfred Granig has over 5 years call center experience. After a year as an agent, Manfred was promoted to Team Leader. He has led both sales and service teams. In 1998, Manfred was the Victorian runner-up for the prestigious Australian Teleservices Association Team Leader of the Year Award. Manfred has participated in developing a call center video for the Commonwealth Bank of Australia with Cohen Brown in the United States.

Frances Gray has worked in the retail and fashion industry for a period of 7 years in various team management and merchandising positions. Frances is currently employed with Zurich Financial Services. She began her career in the Customer Service Call Center. During her time as a Team Manager, Frances used various motivational activities and games. These have proven to help keep her team motivated and enthusiastic. Currently, Frances is working as a Brand Analyst as part of a project team at Zurich Financial Services.

Alex Greenwich, at the age of 19, is the youngest contributor to the book. Nepotism has been a great help to Alex—his mother is the author of *Fun and Gains*, and along with his father, Victor Greenwich, she runs the recruitment and training company where Alex works—Winning Attitudes. Alex is an extremely motivated individual and strives to learn all that he can about the training and recruitment industries. He is currently studying towards a Bachelor of Arts in Human Resource Management at the University of New South Wales. His career goal is to grow with Winning Attitudes, and to help the company to further enhance its excellent reputation. He can be reached by e-mail at *alex@winningattitudes.com*.

Carolyn Greenwich, the author, is a Director of Winning Attitudes, a training and recruitment company that has developed and presented leadership, sales and customer service seminars to over 100 leading companies and organizations. Carolyn is a popular conference presenter on the topics of motivation, sales and customer service. Carolyn's previous book, *The Fun Factor: games, sales contests and activities that make work fun and get results*, was a best seller. If your company is seeking a speaker, please e-mail Carolyn at *carolyn@winningattitudes.com*.

Victor Greenwich is a Director of Winning Attitudes. Victor manages major recruitment projects for call centers for both permanent and temporary sales and service positions. Victor is also very involved in soccer. He is the President of the New South Wales Soccer Coaches Association and Editor of the *Soccer Coaches Journal*. Victor believes that the motivation of the individual or a team—whether on the sports field or in the office—is vital to the success and enjoyment of everyone involved.

Victor Greenwich Jr is a Team Leader and Trainer with Westpac Broking. He has enjoyed 4 years in the call center industry working in insurance, stock broking and technology. His role involves training, management and leadership of his team. Victor believes the secret to success in leadership and motivation is to set a good example, to show respect for colleagues and to have constructive fun at work.

Darren Hauschild has worked in management positions within the call center industry for the last 7 years. He has worked in banking and finance, insurance and energy utilities. While Darren's current title is Head of Direct Sales and Call Centers, over the years he has been responsible for a wide range of issues, including channel migration strategies, marketing management, organizational alignment to new channels and distribution strategies, telephony management, and disaster and business continuity planning together with sales and service management. Darren currently holds the position of Chairperson of the Australian Teleservices Association for the State of South Australia and is a National Director of the Association.

Trevor Harvey has been the Call Center Manager for Australian Wine Selectors in the Hunter Valley for the past 2 years. During this time, the call center has grown from 35 to 120 staff. Trevor has been part of a technology revolution, overseeing the call center change from a manual operation to a full CTI environment. A Marketing Graduate from Newcastle University in the UK, Trevor started his career working for direct marketing agencies in London as an account executive. One of his first assignments was to work on the launch of First Direct (one of the first telephone banking companies). Migrating to Australia in late 1994, Trevor was employed by Telemasters, then the largest outsource teleservice company in Australia. He worked on many major accounts, including Optus, News Ltd and Citibank. From Telemasters, Trevor joined Sitel to work on the Telstra Float as an Operations Manager.

Craig Horley is part of the Investor Service Center team with Colonial First State. His main responsibility is to lead and motivate his team to provide outstanding customer service. He also participates in enhancing procedures and operations and conducting problem-solving investigations. Craig also worked as a part-time manager of a cheesecake shop and service station while completing his Bachelor of Business from the University of Newcastle.

Janeene Hutchinson is a specialist call center manager and consultant with extensive experience in the design, development and management of call center operations. Janeene was a key driver in the establishment of the Optus Vision call center in Brisbane and was responsible for implementing a number of technological advances. As National Manager for FAI's call centers, Janeene implemented a change management program to develop teamwork and introduce a structured approach to rewarding staff. She is a qualified human resource practitioner, and has been responsible for recruitment, selection, industrial management, change management and line management training. Janeene has in-depth experience in managing staff to motivate performance excellence and coaching individual development, resulting in reduced staff attrition and reduced costs.

Susie James Brown has been engaged in marketing- and sales-oriented roles for 11 years in the travel industry. She has developed and managed 2 outbound customer call centers. Her charter for these centers was to employ, train, manage and motivate the staff. Susie takes a positive attitude towards motivating staff, providing opportunities, insuring there is a team spirit and rewarding staff for a job well done. Susie has spent much time focusing on customer service and insuring that every customer receives the information and attention they need to make an informed decision. She feels the two most important factors in business success are dedication to customer service and motivating the customer service team to achieve excellence.

Karen Kearney is the Training and Recruitment Manager at Qantas Corporate Sales. She has a Bachelor of Social Science in Recreation and Tourism. Karen has worked with Qantas for the last 5 years. Starting as an Account Manager, she was responsible for a portfolio of corporate clients. In the last 4 years Karen has been part of the management team. As a team manager she is responsible for the motivation and performance of an outbound sales team.

Paul Kennedy is the Call Center Manager for Rams Direct. Since taking up the role 2 years ago, the center has grown rapidly and was recognized as the Australian Teleservices Association Call Center of the Year (Under 50 People) in 1999. Previously, Paul worked as the Client Service Manager for Commonwealth Securities and was involved in setting up its call center. This center also won the Australian Teleservices Association Call Center of the Year Award (Under 50 People) in 1996. Paul had his start in banking with the St George Bank, where he worked for 17 years in several positions including Customer Service Manager and Telemarketing Manager. In 1992, he won the Silver Management Employee of the Year Award.

Barbara Kernos is Manager of Customer Service for a large bank. She manages a busy call center of approximately 100 staff, which is open 7 days a week. Barbara has over 9 years experience in a variety of positions in both inbound and outbound call centers.

John Knezevic has been involved in the telesales and teleservices industry since 1991, pioneering with three others the Commonwealth Bank's first National Home Loan Hotline. During this time, John has worked in a number of areas, ranging from product management and lending to team leading. Currently, John is Sales Manager for his State. His greatest thrill is to see people live up to their potential and achieve the results they believed were impossible. He believes in giving people a vision and instilling confidence in them. He also encourages a team's determination, drive and desire to succeed. This he believes is the magical formula for success. His center won the prestigious Australian Teleservices Association Call Center of the Year Award in 1998. Two of his team members have won the Australian Teleservices Association Teleprofessional of the Year Award.

Sandra Lau is Call Center and Customer Service Manager for the *Sydney Morning Herald* Classifieds. She has been with the paper since 1978. She started as a Telephone Sales Adviser in an incoming telephone room. Since that time, Sandra has been involved in training and supervizing telephone staff. In 1992, she took on the challenging role of Call Center and Customer Service Manager for 120 staff. Recent challenges have been the relocation of premises without interruption to business and the transformation from a totally inbound center to a mix of both inbound and outbound advertising services. Sandra finds the call center an ever-changing, exciting and evolving environment in which to work.

Elizabeth Lawther is Manager for Training and Development for a major financial institution. As a Training Manager, Elizabeth determines the type of courses and development strategies that the organization puts forward for staff. During the 8 years that she has worked in training, Elizabeth has tried different approaches to learning. She believes that the best way to 'hit the target' is to make learning an enjoyable and fun experience. Elizabeth has found the learning activity that she contributed to *Fun and Gains* to be one of the most successful ways to reinforce learning.

Wayne Lewin is a Team Leader in a bank call center. Wayne has worked for the Commonwealth Bank for over 13 years. Wayne was one of the initial Sales and Service Representatives for the bank's telephone customer service call center. Since being promoted to Team Leader, Wayne has developed a variety of games to help staff achieve a higher level of performance. He believes that 'fun' is a great way to motivate a team.

Seamus Martin has over 15 years call center experience. In 1990, he was part of the management team that set up the first customer service call centers for Optus Communications' mobile telephone service. These centers set the benchmark for call center standards within Australia. After 6 years with Optus, Seamus moved to Pinpoint Marketing, which specializes in developing and managing loyalty programs for companies, primarily within the banking and finance sector. At Pinpoint, Seamus has held the positions of Sales Manager, Preferred Services, and Customer Service Manager, Rewards Programs.

Anna Marsh-Quigley has been involved in telephone sales and customer service for 9 years. She started working as a part-time telemarketer for the National Federation of the Blind while at university. After university, Anna worked as a Phone Floor Manager for an outbound call center that raised money for various charities. Her next career move was to Telstra, where she took a position as a Team Leader for its National Telemarketing Center. For the last 3 years, Anna has worked for the Commonwealth Bank as a Team Leader in home loan sales.

John McCoy-Lancaster brings 10 years of call center experience to his position as the Executive Director of the Australian Teleservices Association. Prior to his appointment in 1999, John was a Professional Development Consultant with Optus Call Center Solutions. During this time, he enhanced call center operations for many blue-chip clients. John has also conducted his own consultancy business, where his highlights were redesigning the Optus induction system for new staff and developing and delivering customer service programs for major organizations. In his position at the Australian Teleservices Association, John aims to further strengthen the association's commitment to the growth and vibrancy of the industry.

Craig MacDonald currently holds the position of Team Leader, Delivery, with the Commonwealth Bank's State Learning Center in Queensland. Within the Commonwealth Bank, Craig has held various positions in the branch network, human resources and call center, and has approximately 8 years experience in a range of learning roles. Outside the Commonwealth Bank, Craig has been actively involved in design and validation committees for TAFE call center course development. He has held positions on industry committees such as the Australian Institute of Banking and Finance QLD Committee, and the Australian Teleservices Association QLD Chapter. Craig has recently completed Certificate IV in Workplace Training and a Bachelor of Commerce with a double major in Organizational Behavior and Human Resource Management, and Industrial Relations. Craig is passionate about learning and follows the motto that 'to learn is to live'.

Muffy McWhinnie is the Director of Power Performance Management, a company that specializes in customer service training. Muffy received her Master's degree in Performing Arts from UCLA, and was then involved in TV and theatre dance productions in Los Angeles and Las Vegas. Her experiences also include working as a complaints manager for a leading plastics company and running her own manufacturing business. She now combines her business experience and knowledge of performance psychology as a complaints management and relationship development trainer. Muffy believes that the 'dance' between the customer and staff is a special performance of its own, requiring well-rehearsed steps to consistently insure positive results.

Narelle Nelson is a Business Manager at Connect Interactive Business Services. Connect Interactive is a teleservice bureau that handles major accounts such as Microsoft, Rams Home Loans and the Sydney Olympics. Prior to taking maternity leave, Narelle was full-time manager on the Sydney Olympics account that took enquiries for tickets, the volunteer program and the torch relay. Previously, Narelle worked in stockbroking for Commonwealth Securities as a Client Service Officer, Team Leader and Client Service Manager. Narelle is currently enjoying a career in motherhood while on maternity leave from Connect Interactive Business Services.

Graeme Newnham started his career in a management capacity several years ago after working with the defense, manufacturing, and gold and diamond industries. Initially he managed 5 networked centers across Australia before taking up his current role with the Commonwealth Bank as Manager of Customer Sales and Service. The balance of achieving business results and creating a positive environment is instantly evident in the center, where several hundred people work hard and have fun every day.

Matthew Oswald currently works as a senior technical writer with a major IT industry distribution firm. Matthew first worked in a call center after studying at the University of Newcastle. Within 3 years he had set up his first inbound and outbound call center with a staff of 15 for a health insurance firm. Matthew enjoys flying, sailing, scuba diving and drinking beer. No one enjoys his occasional turn as a stand-up comic except himself.

Craig Phillips graduated from university with a Bachelor of Economics. Craig worked for AMP in the Fixed Interest Investment Division. Two years later, he started his own financial planning business. Craig's career in the call center industry began when he joined Commonwealth Securities as a Client Service Officer and progressed to Team Leader, and then later joined Connect Interactive Business Services as an Account Manager for the Sydney 2000 Olympics Torch Relay account. Craig is now General Manager and a Director of Office-Pro Productivity Software. This is an Australian company specializing in interactive CD-Rom training for Microsoft Office products. The company's Web site is at *www.office-pro.com.au* and Craig can be reached through e-mail at *craig@office-pro.com.au*.

Lyn Prince has worked in telesales and customer service for 9 years. In her first role, Lyn was responsible for cross-selling additional insurance products that would further benefit the customer. From sales, Lyn moved into customer service and technical service, supporting and assisting new telephone operators when they first started taking telephone calls. For the last 6 years, Lyn has worked in the installment billing department. This position requires meticulous attention to detail and excellent telephone communication skills.

Sherri Prior is currently the Call Center Manager of Jupiters Network Gaming. She began her career with Singapore Airlines in 1984 in the call center. Since that time, Sherri has worked in a number of industries and roles involving customer service and sales linked with the call center or telesales departments. Sherri loves the buzz and excitement of working in a team environment. She has a Diploma in Speech and Drama Teaching and finds this teaching background is invaluable in the day-to-day activity of managing a call center. Sherri cannot imagine working in any other arena and always encourages young people to set their sights on a career in the thriving and growing call center industry.

Mark Pugliese has been with Zurich Insurance since 1995. He began his career as a Customer Service Officer in the personal insurance call center division. Mark also worked in a support role to the Call Center Analyst, which gave him insight how a call center really works. Currently, Mark works as Business Insurance Consultant for the New Business and Retention Division. Mark believes that the most important aspect of the day-to-day functioning of a call center is the happiness of its staff. Staff who work in a stress-free and fun environment make for better and more productive employees. Mark believes that coming up with ideas to maintain interest and perhaps a bit of competition between teams paves the way for a more satisfying work environment.

Judy Purdon has been a Call Center Manager for several years and has worked in sales, sales training and call centers for over 20 years. She has worked in a variety of industries including airlines, banking, insurance, cosmetics and car rentals. Her accomplishments are many, including the establishment of a telemarketing department at Avon that grew from a staff of 4 to 40, and at Avis she set up training and recruitment programs that achieved a significant improvement in workforce morale and stability.

Brenda Shields has been working in the call center industry for 9 years. She started with TeleTech in 1991 as a Customer Service Representative. Since that time, Brenda has worked as Team Leader, Trainer and Operations Manager. She moved to Singapore to help set up and launch TeleTech's new operation there. Brenda has since relocated to the UK where she now is Call Center Operation Manager for ON digital, a large provider of digital TV in the UK. Brenda has managed teams ranging in size from 20 to her current role managing a 560-seat call center. She loves being creative and totally radical in her approach to motivating staff. She has found 'crazy ideas' work well at achieving results. She is passionate about having fun at work.

Frank Speranza worked for 7 years within the branch network of the Commonwealth Bank of Australia, before being selected as part of a group of 30 to launch the Sydney Customer Service Center. Frank's extraordinary success as a sales and service representative was recognized when he won the inaugural 1995 Australian Teleservices Association Teleprofessional of the Year Award. Frank has enjoyed many promotions within the bank and is currently a Team Leader in the Home Lending Division. In 1998, Frank was a finalist for the Australian Teleservices Association Team Leader of the Year Award. Frank loves his job in the call center and feels lucky to work in an industry that is exciting and dynamic.

Mark Stanley has over 8 years experience in the call center industry, concentrated around banking, insurance and financial services. As one of the 'fathers' of the Commonwealth Bank of Australia's telephone and direct banking operation, he gained vast experience in the delivery of sales and service via the telephone in large multi-site call centers. Mark has subsequently held executive call center leadership positions with NRMA in Australia and Citibank N.A. in Singapore, working in 11 countries across Asia Pacific. He is now the Regional Vice-President for Customer

Communication Centers with the American International Group Companies-Japan and Korea. His personal philosophy in relation to high performance call centers is about people, people and people. He believes that creating the right culture and motivation and communication models are the factors that will ultimately differentiate you in the marketplace and give you the business results you seek. While Mark understands the need for world-class technology and process infrastructure, he believes that these are the easier factors to institute in a call center and are the ones that competitors can most easily copy. Mark refers to his teams as 'professional communicators' and works hard at making his people the best.

Cherie Stelzer started work with International Master Publishers as the Training Officer for the Customer Service Division. Cherie was recently promoted to the position of Human Resource Manager. International Master Publishers is a global direct marketing organization that offers collectable information products covering the areas of cooking, craft, family education, health and music. The ideas that Cherie has contributed to the book are the result of fun ideas generated from interested and enthusiastic staff members who have a real drive to always improve. Cherie encourages personal contributions and suggestions during team meetings, project work and training.

Gary Street is the Sales Center Manager at Windscreens O'Brien. Gary has 15 years in the call center industry. He worked for 7 years with American Express and went on to manage call centers for Zurich Insurance and GIO. Gary believes the secret to a fast-paced, high-contact call center is to make the call center a fun place to work. He believes you should treat staff like you want them to treat the customers. Gary is an advocate of the 'hands-on' approach. He believes if you want top performance, you need to spend a lot of time with staff.

Robyn Taylor is a coach and team leader for Centrelink Call Centre in Liverpool. Robyn began as a Customer Service Officer, handling inbound calls about social security benefits. After a year Robyn became a Supervisor, a role she held for 3 years before taking on her current role. Robyn's greatest joy is knowing that she can help other Customer Service Officers at Centrelink to make a difference in the level of customer service that they deliver.

Leon Thompson has worked for the Commonwealth Bank of Australia for 15 years. In 1995, he was part of the team that started the customer service call center in Melbourne. Leon started as a sales and service representative taking 150 calls per day, cross-selling bank products and delivering superior customer service. Leon progressed to Lead Sales and Service Representative before becoming a Team Leader. His team, called 'Leon's Legends', has been highly successful. Because of his success, Leon has been asked to take on the role of Acting Service Manager for the center on a frequent basis, leading 16 teams, each comprising 16 team members.

Tracy Tozer is currently the Deputy Center Manager with NRMA Financial Services. Tracy joined NRMA's branch network in 1989, dealing with customers face to face. After 5 years, Tracy was transferred to NRMA's call center as a Team Leader. As part of her current role, Tracy was given responsibility to increase capacity by 60 seats. The expansion was successfully completed within a limited time frame and under very challenging conditions. By using ideas from *The Fun Factor*, Tracy's team managers have increased the sales focus and results for their center. They have also increased motivation within the center and established a 'fun' working environment.

Craig Tracey is a sales manager with 10 years experience in managing the performance of sales people in both call centers and face-to-face sales. Craig believes the secrets to success are: keep it simple; look after your people; and be inspirational.

Tony Tzoumacas taught high school math for 4 years before joining St George Bank. He started as a Telesales Consultant before being promoted to a Team Leader of the evening team. Tony was then invited to work on several small projects for the Executive Manager of the direct bank to streamline various processes, and increase efficiency and profitability. With this experience behind him, Tony was asked to head up a new outbound team. The objectives of the team were to increase sales within the secured, unsecured and investment areas of the bank. Tony recruited 12 staff members, and developed benchmarks, targets and incentives. Tony was successful in motivating his team to sell and cross-sell the bank's products to existing customers. The game he created, called 'Roulette Royale', proved to be extremely successful. Tony is now a Business Analyst with the bank working on a variety of projects.

Linda Urquhart is a keynote speaker and trainer. Linda develops customized training for local, regional and international clients in the areas of leadership, team building, strategic planning, communication, personality styles and board development. Linda motivates, entertains and educates her audience. Based in Spokane, Washington, Linda has held key roles in the community and State as President of the Pacific Region for the National School Boards Association, the Washington State School Board's Directors Association and the Spokane School Board. Linda holds a Masters degree in Education from Stanford University.

Sarah Wade 'fell' into the call center industry 6 years ago. She thinks it was an accident at the time, but she has never looked back. With 3 years at Telstra and 3 at the Commonwealth Bank of Australia, Sarah has personally grown and enjoyed herself along the way. Sarah is currently a call center manager, and enjoys the challenge and the fun. Coming from a 'training' background, Sarah believes the use of games in the workplace can be critical for staff motivation.

Janelle Wallace has established and managed outbound sales call centers since 1993, in Argentina, Portugal, Spain, the Philippines, Thailand and Australia. Through experience, Janelle has found that there is little difference in outbound selling between countries. All teams need thorough training, motivation and development, as well as professional management. The only difference really is the time it takes to achieve a satisfactory training level. No matter what nationality, sales consultants love games and incentives. All that is needed is to make sure that any cultural sensitivities are taken into account.

Jeannine Walsh is Chief Manager of St George Direct. Jeannine has held various management positions within St George over a 30-year period. Jeannine established St George Direct in 1988, and it is recognized as a leader in telemarketing and customer service within the financial sector of Australia. She is Past-President and a founding member of the Australian Teleservices Association. Jeannine is a regular speaker at both local and national conferences on a range of issues associated with doing business via the telephone, and customer service and staff motivation.

Avril Ward is a Team Manager of Investor Services at Colonial First State Investments. Avril has been with Colonial First State for 5 years, starting as a Super Administrator, and progressing to Investor Service Officer, Team Leader and then Team Manager. Avril is responsible for the day-to-day operation of a busy, fun and fast-growing service center of 25 staff. All staff are multi-skilled in all aspects of the company's products and services. The staff are the most important asset and their feedback is continually sought in order to keep the service center pro-active in providing the services and information the investors require. Colonial First State was a finalist in the 1998 and 1999 Australian Teleservices Association Call Center of the Year Award (Under 50 People).

Sally Wares is the Training Manager of Commonwealth Securities. She joined Commonwealth Securities in January 1999, as she saw an opportunity to join a growing and dynamic company that was establishing itself in a 'field of the future'. Commonwealth Securities is Australia's largest discount stockbroking company, processing around 12 000 to 15 000 trades per day via telephone and the Internet. Prior to this, Sally spent nearly 5 years with BT Funds Management, first as a Client Services Representative and then as a Training Manager in the Client Services Department.

Julianne Wargren has worked in communication and marketing roles. During the last decade, working at a senior level, Julianne has established and managed leading-edge call center bureau services for Telstra and Telemasters and now heads up her own call center consultancy company, W.W. Technology Pty Ltd. Julianne has established call center solutions for most types of call center applications, including inbound and outbound sales and customer service, market research, database cleansing, lead generation and customer satisfaction surveys.

Stacey Watson is Manager of the Telephone Business Center at the NRMA, which employs 200 staff. Stacey started out working in call centers 9 years ago in the banking industry. She worked in telebanking with St George Bank as a consultant, Team Leader and Customer Services Manager. Stacey enjoyed her involvement in establishing and directing new teams and working in IVR scripting and development. Before joining the NRMA, Stacey was Customer Relations Manager with Westpac Financial Services.

Robyn Woodgate has been employed by the Commonwealth Bank of Australia for many years. Prior to having her first child, Timothy, in July 1998, she was Team Leader of the Learning and Development Team at the bank's Sydney customer service center. Robyn has worked with many wonderful people over the years who have taught her a lot. She has learned from experience that an environment that is comfortable and safe is a vital ingredient in the learning process. Another essential ingredient is the element of fun. Robyn's activity, 'Lot of Balls', has helped to break the ice on many occasions and is a great team-building activity.

Bryan Young is a bank manager with 20 years experience in the finance industry. Bryan has worked in retail banking, head office administrations and strategic project management. Bryan progressed from teller to manager to regional manager. He has enjoyed the varied roles that have provided diverse challenges and a plethora of experiences, all within the same organization. Bryan is a committed and highly motivated person who is an exponent of 'motivational and fun' management techniques. Possessed of the theory aspects of management, with qualifications in accounting and an MBA, Bryan believes in pragmatic and innovative techniques to achieve results.